How to Start a Successful Business Without Money and Enjoy Financial Freedom and Happiness

—※—

Bible Based Principles

How to Start a Successful Business Without Money and Enjoy Financial Freedom and Happiness

Bible Based Principles

Chima Amaefula

Scripture quotations marked NLT are taken from the Holy Bible, New Living Translation, copyright ©1996, 2004, 2007 by Tyndale House Foundation. Used by permission of Tyndale House Publishers, Inc., Carol Stream, Illinois, 60188. All rights reserved.
Scripture quotations marked KJV are from the Holy Bible, King James Version (Authorized Version) first published in 1611, and are quoted from the *KJV Classic Reference Bible*, Copyright © 1983 by The Zondervan Corporation.
ISBN: 151210566X
ISBN 13: 9781512105667
Library of Congress Control Number: 2015907518
CreateSpace Independent Publishing Platform
North Charleston, South Carolina

info@biblebasedprinciples.com
www.biblebasedprinciples.com
www.facebook.com/biblebasedprinciples
www.twitter.com/biblebasedprinciples

Available for purchase on Amazon.com,
https://www.createspace.com/5437463, and other retailers.

Dedication

To my lovely wife, Gloria, and my two sons, David and Daniel, for their consistent love and support all through the years, to my Dad, Japhet, for being there for me all through the years and my mother, Victoria, for her consistent prayer and words of blessing for me.

To my dear pastor, Lola Matesun, for believing in me and for being a great source of encouragement. Thank you to Deacon Samson Momoh. I also thank a great man of God and my father and mentor in the Lord, Rev. Dr. Chris Oyakhilome, PhD, for giving me a solid foundation in the Word of God. He taught me that I am who God says I am. I have what God says I have, and I can do what God says I can do. In other words, I know who I am. This is why I can recognize a good gospel message or article when I hear or read one.

A big thank you to Andrew Wommack, for being a great source of inspiration and source of great blessing to me.

Another big thank you to Gaines Hill, Senior Publishing Consultant, CreateSpace, an Amazon company.

Table of contents

Introduction

This book is about the power of the love and grace God offers to anyone who dares to believe Him by simply saying yes to His Word and about how this positive response can give birth to endless possibilities, including starting a successful business without money. I was inspired to write this book to improve people's lives by helping many see how to get a good business idea, how to verify if your business idea will work in the marketplace of life and how to use your idea to start a successful business without money and how doing so is made possible by God's unconditional love, His grace, and faith in His Word. The Bible says, **"But thou shalt remember the LORD thy God: for it is he that giveth thee power to get wealth" (Deut. 8:18 KJV).** It did not say it is money that gives you power to get wealth; rather, it says it is God. One of the powerful ways to get wealth is by having good ideas. And whether you believe it or not, good ideas come from God.

> **Every good gift and every perfect gift is from above, and cometh down from the Father of lights, with whom is no variableness, neither shadow of turning. James 1:17 (KJV).**

It is important to note that God has already done all He's supposed to do for us in every area of our lives (including business) and has already made us an absolute success, but it is left for us to agree with God. **In all thy ways acknowledge him, and he shall direct thy paths (Prov. 3:6 KJV).**

Finding useful information in today's world is much more difficult than ever. There are billions and billions of pages out there, and far too many of them are filled with useless and misleading information. In this book, my goal is to present life-changing information that will position you to take advantage of existing opportunities that God has already given you and to be who God has made you to be in your business life and in every other area of your life. This book fulfills in my life the scripture that says, **"The Lord gave the word, and great were the company that published it" (Ps. 68:11 KJV).** Credit is given to whom credit is due. Everyone quoted in this book deserves a million thanks for the great work they did. My prayer for them is that they will continue to come up with greater works.

When many people think about a business, they have a great vision of selling a wonderful product that will solve problems and give them the freedom to work on something they truly enjoy and that will also give them financial independence they desire so much. But despite their early enthusiasm, sometimes they end up failing to take action. Why?

- They think about the money they need to start the business.
- They have no idea how to start or what to sell.
- They have an idea but are not sure what to do next.
- Fear of failing keeps them from taking action.

Does that sound like you? Don't worry. This book will show you some actionable Bible-based principles for starting your business successfully—and without money.

That may sound impossible to some people, but I know that starting a business without money is possible because I have done it myself. I am a procurement service provider. I started my business without any money, and today it is a very successful business. I started with only an idea, a piece of paper and a pen. I put the three together and created a proposal that I submitted to the people I wanted to serve. Today the rest is a testimony.

In this book, I have enumerated some practical Bible-based principles that made my business a reality. You, too, can take the same steps and get the same results. These powerful principles will always work, whether you are selling a product or offering a service.

The main reason this works is because God's love for us is unconditional. **Long ago the LORD said to Israel: "I have loved you, my people, with an everlasting love. With unfailing love I have drawn you to myself. (Jer. 31:3 KJV). Nay, in all these things we are more than conquerors through him that loved us. (Rom. 8:37 KJV). Since he did not spare even his own Son but gave him up for us all, won't he also give us everything else? (Rom. 8:32 NLT).** God is always on our side supporting us, and He wants us to be very successful in business. Today many Christians don't feel worthy to come to God in faith to ask for whatever they want from Him. They feel that He will not help them because they think that sinful acts in their lives have disqualified them.

Such attitudes do not please God. He doesn't want you to think of Him as the punisher of those who aren't perfect. He wants you to come to Him with an expectation of reward, not because you are good but because He is good. Sin will not stop the power of God working in your life; only unbelief can stop Him **(Hebrews chapter 11 proves this).**

We do not need to do anything to earn God's favor. People who think they need to do something to earn God's favor can never measure up because God's standard is perfection. God loves us because Jesus has paid the price for our sins. All we need to do is trust Jesus (the Word of God), and God will be pleased with us.

Many people are told that God's acceptance and favor are conditional, based on how they perform or whether they measure up to God's standard. This is not what the Bible teaches. God loves you unconditionally and wants you to be successful—not just in your business life, but in all areas of your life.

The gospel as many people present it today causes us to be sin-conscious instead of righteousness-conscious, and it makes us link our salvation and all other blessings from God to our performance. The Bible says this:

For no one can ever be made right in God's sight by doing what his law commands. For the more we know God's law, the clearer it becomes that we aren't obeying it.
But now God has shown us a different way of being right in his sight, not by obeying the law but by the way promised in the scriptures long ago.
We are made right in God's sight when we trust in Jesus Christ to take away our sins. And we all can be saved in this same way, no matter who we are or what we have done (Rom. 3:20–22 NLT).

God's grace has provided not only for salvation but also for every need of your life. God's provision is not based on whether you are reading the Bible enough, praying enough, going to church, or even paying your tithes. That is to say, it is not based on your performance. So being a believer simply means being a believer in the finished works of Jesus Christ for you which includes eternal life as a free gift. Being a believer means believing in God's unconditional love for you that made Him send His only son to die on the cross for you and was resurrected back to life on the third day. Which means His sacrifice for our sins was accepted by God. God's love and mercy towards you has nothing to do with your performance or what you can do for Him. Whatever you do for God is simply your response of trust (faith) in Him and thanksgiving for His unconditional love for you. It is not about your performance; it is about your faith in Jesus and what He has done for you.

Before you ever had a financial need, God created the provision for it **(2Cor. 8:9).** Before you were sick, God through grace provided your healing **(1 Pet. 2:24).** Before you ever became discouraged, God blessed you with all spiritual blessings **(Eph. 1:3).** God anticipated every need you could ever have and met those needs through Jesus before you existed. That's grace. Starting a business successfully without money is one of those needs God has provided for, and this book shows you how to recognize this provision in your life and take advantage of it.

Jesus said unto him, if thou canst believe, all things are possible to him that believeth (Mk. 9:23 KJV).
And ye shall know the truth, and the truth shall make you free (Jn. 8:32 KJV).

Note that having plenty of money is not prosperity; money is the by-product of prosperity. The real asset is the favor of God, which brings the ideas, ability, knowledge, talent and visions that bring the money. This book shows you how you already have both the favor of God and earth-shaking business ideas inside you and shows you how to turn these ideas into money.

Having plenty of money may give you some degree of financial security but not financial freedom. Financial security without trust in God is not freedom but bondage and uncertain riches. **In the Bible, 1 Timothy 6:17 puts it this way: "Charge them that are rich in this world, that they be not high-minded, nor trust in uncertain riches, but in the living God, who giveth us richly all things to enjoy." (KJV).** The enjoyment in the above scripture includes financial freedom that comes from God. It happens only when we put our trust in the living God and not in uncertain riches.

The first step to financial freedom is recognizing that you are a steward of God's finances. This requires a huge mind set shift from the way the world views money. The world encourages you to be an owner and not a steward. But it's not up to you to choose what you do with your finances because God owns you and your finances. The question is why does God want us to give to Him since He owns everything that we have? The answer is that God is a spirit and requires your faith (trust) in Him to protect your finances from the enemy who comes to steal, kill and destroy you. God has given you finances so that you'll trust Him with them. Then He will cause you to enjoy financial freedom. I know that sounds too good to be true, but it is.

It is also important to note that a person can own the most successful business in the world and still not be happy and contented. Why is that? Because happiness isn't a state of being; it's a state of mind. **And he said unto them, Take heed, and beware of covetousness: for a man's life**

consisteth not in the abundance of the things which he possesseth. (Lk. 12:15 KJV)

A person can be happy when everyone and everything around him or her is in turmoil. People can be content no matter what their financial or physical conditions might be. True happiness and contentment are not dependent on circumstances. It is a choice.

Today, many people think happiness is a result of what happens to them instead of a choice. They believe that if they didn't have any problems and if they had an abundance of good things, happiness would be the inevitable result. That's not true.

This book will show you how to start a successful business without money and enjoy financial freedom and how to be happy in life. It will transform, in a positive way, the way you see God, the way you see money, the way you relate to God and the way you receive from God.

Be assured that this book will deliver on its promises because it is based on God's word which cannot fail. When it blesses you, kindly obtain copies for your loved ones and recommend it to as many people as possible so they can also be blessed by it. Happy reading!

Chapter One

You've Already Got Earth-Shaking Business Ideas inside You

What kind of ideas do you want God to give you? The truth is, you don't need God to give you any ideas. He's already done His part. Whatever ideas you need, you already have them.

This may sound unreasonable to you. You might be thinking, "But I have no ideas. You don't know me." But regardless of what the natural facts are, the truth is that God has already given you whatever ideas you need to succeed in this world.

According as His divine power hath given unto us all things that pertain unto life and godliness, through the knowledge of Him that hath called us to glory and virtue (2 Pet. 1:3 KJV).

The Only Thing We Are Lacking Is Knowledge

Most Christians believe God can do anything, but many of them don't believe He has done very much. They live in a constant state of trying to get God to do something. They are begging God to move in their lives. They run from meeting to meeting, trying to get something from God. But they already have it.

Blessed be the God and father of our Lord Jesus Christ, who hath blessed us with all spiritual blessings in heavenly places in Christ (Eph. 1:3 KJV).

The above scripture says, "He hath blessed us with all spiritual blessings." This means it's already done—including that business idea you desire to implement. You have it inside of you; it just needs to be activated. You already have all spiritual blessings, so asking God or waiting on Him to bless you is counterproductive. Yet the average Christian starts from this position whenever he or she needs anything from God.

For instance, if their bodies are sick, they don't start from, "By His stripes, I was healed" **(1 Pet. 2:24)** or from "I have the same power (the Holy Spirit) that raised Jesus from the dead living in me" **(Eph. 1:19–20)**. Instead, they will focus on the doctor's report or the pain in their bodies and say, "I'm sick, God will You heal me?" They start moving toward victory instead of coming from victory.

Never try to make God do something He has already provided. It will never work. Simply receive what He has already provided.

If you didn't understand this, then I can guarantee you that this is one of the main reasons you haven't been receiving from God. You need to get a revelation of this. Jesus has already provided everything you will ever need. You are blessed with all spiritual blessings—all of them, including supernatural, earth-shaking business ideas.

Whether or not we see a physical manifestation of what God has done in the spiritual realm depends on what we believe and how we act, not on what God needs to do. For instance, it's not up to the Lord to heal us. He has already healed us **(1 Pet. 2:24).** In the same way, God has already given us great business ideas. It's left for us to receive them.

Everything we will ever need in our lives has already been provided. You've got to start from the idea that "God has already provided everything, and if I can't see it, it's not that God didn't give; it's that I don't realize what I have." When you know you have something, it takes the struggle, fear, and worry out of it. It takes you out of the condemnation that says you are not worthy of God's blessings. It takes you out of the legalistic mentality of trying to earn things from God. It removes doubt. How could you ever doubt that you didn't get something you already have? It's really that simple. Again, let's look at **Ephesians 1:3.**

> **Blessed be the God and father of our Lord Jesus Christ, who** *hath* **[past tense] blessed us with all spiritual blessing in heavenly place in Christ (KJV, emphasis mine).**

As you can see, those spiritual blessings are in heavenly places in Christ, but they are in you because you are in Christ, which is what the next verse says.

> **According as He hath chosen us in him before the foundation of the world (Eph. 1:4 KJV).**

Philemon 6 also explains this truth. Paul was praying "that the communication of thy faith may become effective." That means that your faith would begin to work "by the acknowledging of every good thing that is in you in Christ Jesus." You see, every good thing is in you in Christ! You already have it. And He said He would never leave you nor forsake you **(Heb. 13:5).**

Just start acknowledging the good things the Word of God says are in you, including supernatural business ideas, and then your faith will begin to be effective. You will start seeing these things manifest in your life. This is so much easier than begging and pleading with God to do it. This is the Bible-based way of getting good and great ideas. Just acknowledge that you already have them, and they will manifest in you. God has already done His part. When Jesus died on the cross, He said, "It is finished" **(John 19:30).**

> **I pray that you will begin to understand the incredible greatness of His power for us who believe him. This is the same mighty power that raised Christ from the dead and seated him in the heavenly realms (Eph. 1:19–20 NLT).**

He is not working anymore. He has already done it. It is finished. Do you need earth-shaking business ideas? It has already been done. Jesus did it for you more than two thousand years ago. Do you need to be saved?

He is the sacrifice for our sins. He takes away not only our sins but the sins of all the world (1 John 2:2 NLT).

He has already forgiven the sins of the entire world. It is not a matter of whether God will forgive you. He's already forgiven your sins. Will you receive His forgiveness and put your faith in what Jesus has done? That's all you need to do.

God has already given you supernatural business ideas. He has already forgiven you. He has already healed you. He has already blessed your business and finances. He has already given you love, joy, and peace. You don't need God to respond to you; you need to learn to respond to God! It's easier to defend something you already have than to go and get something you don't have.

This is so powerful, but it is what so many Christians are missing. They know God can do anything they want, but they don't think He has done anything yet. They start from a position of unbelief.

Death and life are in the power of the tongue (Prov. 18:21 KJV).

We must release the power of God that is already on the inside of us. You must say to yourself, "I have supernatural business ideas inside of me." This is how you start cooperating with God—by seeing yourself the way God sees you and by boldly saying the same to yourself.

We need to begin to believe that things have happened that we can't see, taste, hear, smell, or feel. We believe there are television and radio signals in the atmosphere, even though we can't see them. We know that all we have to do is take a television set, turn it on, and tune it in, and we will see that those signals were there the whole time. We need to begin to apply this belief to spiritual things. We can't limit this concept to just our physical realm.

There is more going on around you than just what you can perceive with your five senses. There is a spirit on the inside of you, and there is a spiritual realm where God has already done His part. You need to live from the standpoint that God has already done it. He has provided everything you need.

It is not a matter of trying to get God to move in your life. It's a matter of you moving over into agreement with Him and receiving what He has already provided.

Ideas from God Are Supernatural Ideas

There are "good ideas," and there are "God ideas." Some people have good ideas that may not necessarily yield results at the end of the day, but when it is a "God idea" given to you by God himself, you can be sure it will defeat all the odds. God always gives His children earth-shaking money-making ideas!

The pharaoh had a dream one day that troubled him. He saw seven lean cows swallow up seven fat cows. He also saw seven diseased ears of corn consume seven healthy ones. When none of his wise men could interpret the dream, someone remembered a Hebrew prisoner called Joseph **(Gen. 41).** Joseph came and interpreted the dream, which signified seven years of plenty and seven years of famine. That was nice, but it didn't answer the question "What do we do about it, Joseph?" Joseph replied as follows:

> **My suggestion is that you find the wisest man in Egypt and put him in charge of administering a nationwide farm program. Let Pharaoh appoint officials over the land, and let them collect one-fifth of all the crops during the good seven years. Have them gather all the food and grain of these good years into the royal storehouses and store it away so that there will be food in the cities. That way there will be enough to eat when the seven**

years of famine come. Otherwise disaster will surely strike the land, and all the people will die (Gen. 41:33–36 NLT).

How come nobody else came up with an idea like that? Such an idea could have come only from God. At the end of the day, Egypt was preserved, and Joseph quickly became very influential. When God gives you an idea, it's more valuable than money. His supernatural ideas will make money and favor gravitate toward you because His ideas will always change the status quo. What God did for Joseph, He has also done for every one of us.

Then Peter opened his mouth, and said, of a truth I perceive that God is no respecter of persons (Acts 10:34 KJV).

Open your heart and mind to receive a God idea for your business, education, marriage, family, and life today.

Chapter Two

Our Words Have Power to Make or Break Us

If we want to start seeing the power of God manifest in our lives, we will have to start paying attention to what we say. Words have power—more than any of us realize—but we often speak them as though they are meaningless. Because of that, most believers at one time or another have been *hung by their tongue*.

But I say unto you, that every idle word that men shall speak, they shall give account thereof in the day of judgment. For by thy words thou shalt be justified, and by thy words thou shalt be condemned (Matt. 12:36–37 KJV).

"Every idle word" simply means words that are nonproductive. These are words you speak but don't believe. For example, you might say, "I can't start a successful business without money." Such statement places limitations on you.

Every time you say things you don't really mean, it begins to numb your heart. Unconsciously, each idle word is making it just a little bit harder to believe that what you say will actually come to pass when you mean it and it really counts.

Jesus certainly understood the power of words, and He used them to change the natural things around Him.

And seeing a fig tree afar off having leaves, he came, if haply he might find anything thereon: and when he came to it, he found nothing but leaves; for the time of figs was not yet.
And Jesus answered and said unto it, no man eat fruit of thee hereafter forever. And his disciples heard it... (MK. 11:12-14 KJV)
And in the morning, as they passed by, they saw the fig tree dried up from the roots.
And Peter calling to remembrance saith unto him, Master, behold, the fig tree which thou curseth is withered away.
And Jesus answering saith unto them, Have faith in God.
For verily I say unto you, That whosoever shall say unto this mountain, Be thou removed, and be thou cast into the sea; and shall not doubt in his heart, but shall believe that those things which he saith shall come to pass; he shall have whatsoever he saith. Therefore I say unto you,
What things soever ye desire, when ye pray, believe that ye receive them, and ye shall have them. (MK 11:20-24 KJV)

Jesus was amazed at his unbelief. He was saying, "It shouldn't shock you to see this tree withered. Have faith in God."

Then He went on to explain that this phenomenon wasn't limited to a fig tree. He used a mountain as an example, but I believe it could apply to anything. He was making the point that if we say it with our mouths and believe it in our hearts, we can have what we say.

He also made it very clear who qualified to use words in this way. He said, "Whosoever shall say." Are you a whosoever? If you are and if you're breathing, then you're qualified, and your words can affect the natural world as well as the spiritual world.

Jesus used the word "say" or "saith" three times in verse 23. He was making it clear that words have power. But He also said to have faith in God. The words that have power are words that are filled with faith. And it's important to understand that the faith they're filled with is not your human faith.

I am crucified with Christ: nevertheless I live; yet not I, but Christ liveth in me: and the life which I now live in the flesh I live by the faith of the Son of God, who loved me, and gave himself for me (Gal. 2:20 KJV).

This is talking about *the very faith of God* that He placed in you when you were born again. In fact, you can't even be born again by your own faith. **Romans 10:17** says that faith comes by the word, and **1 Peter 1:23** says you are born again by the Word of God.

If we can't even believe in salvation with our human faith, how could we possibly use it for other things like healing or prosperity? It's extremely important that you understand this. If you don't know this, you will always be looking to others to pray for you. You'll always think that they have more faith than you do, and because of that, God will act on your behalf when they pray. That's wrong, and it's the reason many Christians are looking to humanity instead of God for their answers.

For I say, through the grace given unto me, to every man that is among you, not to think of himself more highly than he ought to think; but to think soberly, according as God hath dealt to every man *the measure* of faith (Rom. 12:3 KJV).

Think of it like using a spoon to dish up soup. If you used the same spoon every time—and God did—every person will get the same amount of soup. It's the *measure* of soup. You have the measure of faith. No born-again believer has more faith than any other; some just do a better job of appropriating what they have been given.

Now faith is the substance of things hoped for, the evidence of things not seen....
Through faith we understand that the worlds were framed by the Word of God, so that things which are seen were not made of things which do appear (Heb. 11:1 and 3 KJV).

This scripture is not symbolic; God actually created everything with words. He spoke creation into existence, and the substance of His faith manifested into what we can now see. The Word of God has unlimited power. Each word is like a little capsule filled with faith waiting for us believers to release it in our hearts and speak it with our mouths.

Everything we see was created by words, and it is the very Word of God that holds the universe together **(Heb. 1:3).** Therefore, everything we see will respond to faith-filled words. They have to respond because words are the parent force. **Proverbs 23:7** says that as you think in your heart, so are you, and **Luke 6:45** says that what you speak comes from the abundance of your heart. In other words, the way you think controls the way you talk. And if you understand that your words have power, then you understand why you can be hung by your tongue.

The only reason every one of us isn't dead from the many idle words we have spoken is because we haven't believed every one of those words with our hearts. Thank God that our words have to be mixed with faith and that we have to believe them from our hearts. But this should help us see a powerful truth. If we believe we are going to be sick or if we believe that we will always be poor or cannot make it in business and then confess that with our mouths, we will get what we believe.

On the other hand, what happens when we take the faith-filled words of God and plant them in our hearts, where they can take root and grow? Everything changes! No longer are we just saying, "I believe that I'm healed" or "I am prosperous," but we believe it, *and the faith of God* is then released through those words.

Death and life are in the power of the tongue: and they that love it shall eat the fruit thereof (Prov. 18:21 KJV).

It says not only life but death as well. It's sad to say, but most of the words being communicated today are negative words—words that do not bring about abundant life but cause more problems.

It's Our Responsibility to Keep Ourselves in God's Blessing with Our Mouths

> **We all make mistakes, but those who control their tongues can also control themselves in every other way.**
> **We can make a large horse turn around and go wherever we want by means of a small bit in its mouth.**
> **And a tiny rudder makes a huge ship turn wherever the pilot wants it to go, even though the winds are strong.**
> **So also, the tongue is a small thing, but what enormous damage it can do. A tiny spark can set a great forest on fire (James 3:2–5 NLT). Today I have given you the choice between life and death, between blessing and curses. I call on heaven and earth to witness the choice you make. Oh, that you would choose life, that you and your descendants might live! (Deut. 30:19 NLT).**

Through your confession, you can choose what you want your life to be. Your mouth is the key that'll unlock the blessings of God in your life! You can open the doors of prosperity and blessing in your life with your mouth, and with the same mouth you can introduce poverty, death, and curses as well.

> **For he that will love life, and see good days, let him refrain his tongue from evil, and his lips that they speak no guile (1 Pet. 3:10 KJV).**

Though your tongue is small, it controls everything in your life. With it, you can chart your course unto a prosperous life. God has given us the keys to riches, and that means we can use our mouths to unlock doors of blessing.

> **And I will give you the keys of the Kingdom of Heaven. Whatever you lock on earth will be locked in heaven, and whatever you open on earth will be opened in heaven (Matt. 16:19 NLT).**

Note that you lock and unlock with your mouth.

But the way of getting right with God through faith says, "You don't need to go to heaven" (to find Christ and bring him down to help you),
And it says, "You don't need to go to the place of the dead" (to bring Christ back to life again).
Salvation that comes from trusting Christ—which is the message we preach—is already within easy reach. In fact, the Scriptures say, "The message is close at hand; it is on your lips and in your heart" (Rom. 10:6–8 NLT).

Therefore, you have to fill your heart with God's Word.

You brood of snakes! How could evil men like you speak what is good and right? For whatever is in your heart determines what you say.
A good person produces good words from a good heart, and an evil person produces evil words from an evil heart. (Matt. 12:34–35 NLT).

As you can see, it's not about your level of education, your connections, or your skills and talents. These things are important, no doubt, but what really matters in life is the condition of your heart and the words you speak as a result. This is what will determine your ultimate success or failure. Success here means all-around success—not to be a success in one area of your life but a failure in other areas.

A wholesome tongue is a tree of life; but perverseness therein is a breach in the spirit (Prov. 15:4 KJV).
For verily I say unto you, that whosoever shall say unto this mountain, be thou removed, and be thou cast into the sea, and

shall not doubt in his heart, but shall believe that those things which he saith shall come to pass, he shall have whatsoever he saith.

Therefore I say unto you, what things soever ye desire, when ye pray, believe that ye receive them, and ye shall have them (Mark 11:23–24 KJV).

The words you say as a man or woman who has received the Holy Spirit are words of power. Every day take time to prophesy about your day. Use your tongue to order the circumstances of your life correctly. As you speak or confess God's Word, the Holy Spirit does something beautiful for you: He causes the anointing to well up strongly within you. At such times, the words you speak go forth as the sword of the Spirit of God. They become the *rhema* word by which you cut down and overcome every adversity or situation. Hallelujah!

The Spirit of Faith Speaks What It Wants to See and Receives It

We having the same spirit of faith, according as it is written, I believed, and therefore have I spoken; we also believe, and therefore speak (2 Cor. 4:13 KJV).

In this scripture, the spirit of God shows us the major characteristic of the spirit of faith: it believes and therefore speaks. In other words, when you're operating by the spirit of faith, you don't speak or confess something to make it happen, nor do you try to convince yourself that what you're saying exists. Rather, you believe first in your heart that what you desire exists before you give voice to it.

This is where some misunderstand faith. They're not speaking because they've believed; they're speaking to believe. Though they're confessing

God's Word, they're actually struggling to believe what they're saying. This explains why they get frustrated when things don't turn out as they expected.

The Lord said this to Abram:

"Neither shall thy name any more be called Abram, but thy name shall be Abraham; for a father of many nations have I made you" (Gen. 17:5 KJV).

At this time, the man was still childless, but because he had the spirit of faith, he immediately began to call himself Abraham ("father of many"). He didn't wait to see the physical children before he confessed who God called him. He believed, and therefore he spoke out that he was the father of many. That's the spirit of faith at work.

As it is written, I have made thee a father of many nations, before him whom he believed, even God, who quickeneth the dead, and calleth those things which be not as though they were.
And being not weak in faith, he considered not his own body now dead, when he was about an hundred years old, neither yet the deadness of Sarah's womb:
He staggered not at the promise of God through unbelief; but was strong in faith, giving glory to God;
And being fully persuaded that, what he had promised, he was able also to perform.
And therefore it was imputed to him for righteousness.
Now it was not written for his sake alone, that it was imputed to him,
But for us also, to whom it shall be imputed, if we believe on him that raised up Jesus our Lord from the dead;
Who was delivered for our offences, and was raised again for our justification (Rom. 4:17–25 KJV).

Faith is the evidence that what you hoped for is now a reality (**Heb. 11:1**), and that's why your confession must be based on what you've believed in your heart, not the other way around. If you have evidence of something, it gives you the confidence to speak of it boldly. For example, if you have documents that prove you own a certain property, you will laugh at anyone who claims ownership of that same property. Why? The proof is with you!

In the same way, when you believe that what God has said about you is a reality, you're bold to declare it, notwithstanding what the devil, circumstances, and even your mind may tell you. That's because you have the knowledge in your spirit. The proof that those things are real is inside you! That's functioning by the spirit of faith.

There's no situation that can't be changed and no sickness in your body that can't be healed. You can cause a change by making your tongue your own tree of life by declaring God's Word over your life and situation. The fact that you can walk out of misery, poverty, lack, depression, unhappiness, and even death is simply exciting. You can walk out of anything that demeans you today. All you need do is to get into the good life by using your tongue right, and your life will change. This includes your business life.

Note that all creation has intelligence.

And he arose, and rebuked the wind, and said unto the sea, peace, be still. And the wind ceased, and there was a great calm (Mark 4:39 KJV).

All of creation, both living and nonliving, has intelligence. This is very clear in the Word of God. Jesus talked to the wind, to water, to bread, to fish, and even to trees. He talked to the blind, the lame, the deaf, the mentally deranged, and to the dead. In the Old Testament, the Lord instructed Ezekiel to prophesy to the bones. When he did so, the Bible says that there was a noise and the bones came together, bone to its bone (**Ezek. 37:1–7**).

The bones did not just hear words. They had the intelligence of memory such that, even though they had been detached from each other for a long time, at the word of Ezekiel, every bone knew exactly which bone to connect to. No bone belonging to Mr. A went to Mr. B. Every bone went to its original owner. That's some intelligence!

Everything has intelligence because in the beginning, God created everything with His words. The Word of God designed them to retain intelligence. The things God made had to hear God before they could respond to His instructions. For instance, when He commanded the water to bring forth fishes from the sea, the water retained the "programming" and produced the fishes. Thus, both the water and the fishes that came out of it were connected to the programming of God's Word. If humans could program things that are nonliving and retain that programming, how much more can God, Who created humans, do?

By talking to these elements, God communicated and programmed energy into them, and they retained it. Now you can understand why we must speak by the anointing of the Spirit of God in us because the Spirit of God helps us program the right meaning into our words. Speak to your body, your car, your property, your business, and everything connected to you, for they all have intelligence. Speak what you want to see happen in any area of your life, and it shall be so. Remember, your mouth was given to you not just to eat and drink but to chart your way in life and to program your life from success to success. The ideas you need to start a successful business are already inside you, call them forth today, without giving up, and you shall have them. Say to yourself I have good ideas and I receive them for a successful business in Jesus name. Amen.

Chapter Three

Grace and Faith Work Together to
Deliver God's Best to You

Most people ask, "What do I need to do to receive the blessings of God? I have been praying, reading the Bible, going to church, paying my tithes, and giving my offerings, yet I don't seem to be able to get my prayers answered."

In that question lies the root of the problem. Sometimes people fall into the trap of thinking that God responds to their needs according to their performance. They have not properly understood the balance of grace and faith—and their relationship with each other.

By basic definition, the word "grace" means "unmerited, unearned, underserved favor." The good news is that grace has nothing to do with you. Grace existed before you ever come to be. Another way to say it is that grace is God's part.

"Faith" is defined as a positive response of the human spirit to what God has already provided by grace. In other words, faith is your positive response to God's grace, or faith appropriates what God has already provided for you. Therefore, faith is your part.

Grace and faith work together, and they must be in balance.

For by Grace are ye saved through faith and that not of yourselves:
It is the gift of God: not of works, lest any man should boast (Eph. 2:8–9 KJV).

This verse declares a profound truth. It says we are saved by grace through faith, not through one or the other. Think of it this way: grace is what God does, while faith is what we do. It takes both working together to receive salvation.

Salvation is not dependent on grace alone. If it were, everyone would be saved and go to heaven, for God's grace is the same toward everyone.

For the Grace of God that bringeth salvation hath appeared to all men (Titus 2:11 KJV).

God has already given the gift of salvation to everyone through Jesus. It is by faith that a person receives what was done more than two thousand years ago.

Most people believe that to be saved, we need to ask God to forgive us of our sins, but that isn't what the Bible teaches.

And he is the propitiation for our sins and not for ours only, but also for the sins of the whole world (1 John 2:2 KJV).

Jesus didn't die just for those He knew would accept Him; He died for every sinner who has ever lived on this earth. And He died before you or I ever committed a single sin. Sin is not an issue with God. The Lord isn't waiting for us to ask Him to forgive us for our sins. The sins of the entire world—past, present, and future—have already been forgiven. God has already done His part. It is now up to you to receive the truth by faith and make it a reality in your life.

Behold the Lamb of God, which taketh away the sin of the world (John 1:29 KJV).
And when he is come, he will reprove the world of sin and of righteousness, and of judgment: of sin, because they believe not on me (John 16:8–9 KJV).

The Holy Spirit is not on earth to convict people of their sins. The Holy Spirit is here to convict people of the single sin of not receiving Jesus as their savior. People do not go to hell for committing adultery, stealing, or even committing murder. These, like all sins, have already been paid for. This is what the Bible says in **John 16:8–9.** The only sin that is going to send people to hell is the sin of rejecting Jesus Christ as their personal savior. So stop magnifying sin in your life.

Jesus hasn't saved, healed, delivered, or prospered a single person in the past two thousand years. What God provided by grace more than two thousand years ago now becomes a reality when mixed with faith. Faith appropriates what God has already provided. Our faith doesn't move God; He isn't the one who is stuck. Faith doesn't make God do anything. Grace and faith work together, and our part is to accept what God has already done. Grace must be balanced with faith.

Some Christians believe that God moves sovereignly as He wills, when He wills. That is because religion teaches that God controls everything and that nothing can happen without His permission. That is not true; not everything is up to God.

God is being misrepresented. If He were guilty of all the things some people blame Him for, there wouldn't be a civilized nation on the face of this earth that wouldn't convict Him of crimes against humanity. The idea that God either causes or allows evil so that we will somehow grow spiritually is the worst heresy in the body of Christ. It renders people passive and takes away their ability to resist the devil.

If you really believe that God controls everything, what's the use of doing anything? After all, it's all up to God, right? If you believe that God is trying to teach you something through sickness or poverty, why see a doctor or look for a good job? Why not suffer as much as you can and really learn the lesson?

This is a terrible doctrine. The Bible says that in the last days, people will call evil good and good evil **(Isa. 5:20).** Some people today are teaching the idea that when you get sick or experience financial problems, God is causing it so that He can teach you something or humble you. That is an example of calling evil good.

God is not responsible for killing babies or for rape, violence, poverty, or sickness. Satan is the author of evil, and the Bible clearly states that we are to resist the enemy **(James 4:7).** To resist means to actively fight against something. If we aren't fighting against sickness, for example, then we are submitting to it. To casually say to Satan, "Please leave us alone" is not resisting the devil. We need to get angry at the devil, and we won't get angry if we believe that God is the one causing or allowing the problem.

God's will doesn't automatically come to pass. Jesus said that not everybody would be saved **(Matt. 7:13),** yet scripture says it is the will of God that none should perish **(2 Pet. 3:9).** God has provided salvation, healing, financial provision, and everything else we need, but if we don't respond in faith to what He has provided by grace, we won't receive.

God's will is for everyone to be healed. **Acts 10:38** says Jesus went about doing good and healing all who were oppressed by the devil, and it calls what He did "good." In **1 Peter 2:24,** it says we were healed by His stripes, yet most of us still do not receive His healing into our lives.

It is not the truth that sets you free; it is the truth you know and act on that will set you free **(John 8:32).** The truth is that you need to put your faith in what God has already done rather than in what you do. God, by His grace, has already provided healing, prosperity, forgiveness for sin, and much more. However, all of that must be appropriated by faith.

God has done His part by giving us His son, Jesus. His grace has provided everything through the sacrifice of Jesus. This is nearly too good to be true; there is absolutely nothing we can do to earn it and nothing we can do to lose it. Our part is simple: we respond to His grace by faith and appropriate what has already been accomplished. Most Christians don't understand this concept. Make sure you are not among them. This is the foundation of your relationship with God and the reason you feel that God is not answering your prayers.

Grace without your positive response of faith won't save you, and faith that isn't a response to God's grace will bring you into condemnation. Put your faith in what God has already done for you, and you will have the victory that overcomes the world **(1 John 5:4 KJV).**

The Difference between Religion and Christianity

In one word the answer is grace or the unconditional love of God. Grace means undeserved or unmerited favor of God.

The wrath of God is revealed from heaven against all ungodliness and unrighteousness of men, who hold the truth in unrighteousness.

Because that which may be known of God is manifest in them; for God hath shewed it unto them.
For the invisible things of him from the creation of the world are clearly seen, being understood by the things that are made, even his eternal power and Godhead; so that they are without excuse (Rom. 1:18–20 KJV).

Ever since the fall of Adam, humanity has been trying to find a way back to God. There is a longing within every person to be back in the image that God created him or her in. We have knowledge that there must be something more. The religions of the world are a testimony to this scripture, but from the first chapter of Romans, we can see that God has revealed Himself to His creation. But humanity has devised nearly as many different ways to approach God as there have been people.

The difference between religion and Christianity is basically that religion is humanity's attempt to reach God, but Christianity is God reaching out to humans and then living in humans. Christianity is the pulsating life of God in a man or woman.

Christianity is the grace of God towards man. It is unmerited and undeserved favor of God offered to man unconditionally. It is only Christianity that offers salvation to man unconditionally. All the religions of the world fall short of obtaining salvation because they put the burden of salvation on humanity. They teach that through our adherence to a rigid standard of dos and don'ts, we make ourselves acceptable to God. But God revealed in **James 2:10** that if you keep the whole law and yet offend in one point, you are guilty of all. This is where the religions of the world have missed it.

They have all sinned, and they all come short of the glory of God **(Rom. 3:23)**. Humanity cannot save itself; it has to have a savior.

So God sent His son, Jesus, in the likeness of sinful flesh to condemn sin in the flesh that we might come into right standing with God **(Rom. 8:3–4)**. We are made acceptable to God through who Jesus is and what He did **(Eph. 1:6)**. Jesus said of Himself that He is the only way unto the Father **(John 14:6)**. Peter said in **Acts 4:12, "Neither is there salvation in any other: for there is none other name under heaven given among men, whereby we must be saved."** God is the only one Who could provide salvation for humanity—through Jesus. And any other attempts to approach God, regardless of how sincere they may be, will end in total failure, with the result of eternal death.

> **Master, which is the great commandment in the law? Jesus said unto him, thou shalt love the Lord thy God with all thy heart, and with all thy soul, and with all thy mind. This is the first and great commandment. And the second is like unto it, thou shalt love thy neighbor as thy self (Matt. 22:36 KJV).**

Jesus revealed that all of the Old Testament laws were designed to instruct us how to love God and others. Therefore, the two commands that dealt directly with loving God and others **(Lev. 19:18 and Deut. 6:5)** were the most important. The religious leaders had become so obsessed with keeping every minor detail of the law that they had lost sight of its ultimate purpose. They loved neither God nor other people, yet they thought they were keeping the law.

The same thing is happening today. Some of the cruelest acts of people toward others have been done in the name of the Lord by people who thought they were defending God's holy commandments. However, if we violate one of the two greatest commandments in an effort to enforce some other commandment, then we are misapplying God's Word, just as these religious Jews did.

The Old Testament law and the New Testament concept of grace compel people to the same end—that is, to love God and their fellow humans. However, the motivations to this end are different. The Old Testament law motivated people to love God and others through fear of punishment if they failed to comply. The New Testament concept of grace freely gives us a godlike kind of love that is unconditional and tells us to love others as we are loved by God.

It is possible to display actions of holiness but not love God. It is impossible for God's kind of love not to produce holiness. Holiness is a fruit, not the root, of loving.

> **But woe unto you, Pharisees! For ye tithe mint and rue and all manner of herbs, and pass over judgment and the love of God: these ought ye to have done and not to leave the other undone (Luke 11:42 KJV).**

When Jesus said, "and not to leave the other undone," it is clear that He is not arguing against doing what is right. God's Word stresses holiness in our actions. The Pharisees' error that caused Jesus's rebuke was that they believed their actions could produce the right relationship with God. But a proper relationship with God can come only by humbling ourselves and putting faith in a savior, who is Jesus. God cleanses our hearts by grace through faith **(Eph. 2:8)**, and then we have our fruit unto holiness **(Rom. 6:22)**. Again, holiness is a fruit, not the root, of salvation.

A similar instance is found in **Matthew 23:26**. Jesus told the Pharisees, "Thou blind Pharisee, cleanse first that which is within the cup and platter that the outside of them may be clean also." True Christianity comes from the inside out. A good heart will change someone's actions, but a person's actions cannot change his or her heart.

One of religion's favorite doctrines is that if you will just act right, you will be right. Nothing could be further from the truth. You must be born again and receive the Holy Spirit. Let Him lead you. And if you are born again, then holiness is a by-product, not the way to a relationship with God.

This is the heart of the gospel. Every major religion of the world has a moral standard it enforces, but only Christianity offers salvation unconditionally through a savior. Presenting holiness in any way other than as a result of salvation is denying Jesus as our savior and places the burden of salvation on us. Improper emphasis on achieving holiness or salvation through a person's own actions can damn that person. We must trust Jesus completely.

And when the Pharisee saw it, he marveled that he had not first washed before dinner (Luke 11:38 KJV).

A sure sign of the error of legalism is misplaced priorities, as we see here with these Pharisees. It is not recorded in scripture that the Pharisees marveled at the wonderful works of Jesus; they were too busy looking for something to criticize **(Mark 3:2)**. But they marveled at Jesus not washing His hands. This is a classic example of straining out a gnat and swallowing a camel **(Matt. 23:24)**.

Those who seek to earn righteousness through keeping the law are consumed with "doing," while those who receive righteousness by faith are simply confessing what has already been done. This is a simple yet profound difference. If we are still "doing" acts of holiness to get God to move in our lives, then we are still operating under a "law" mentality that is not faith **(Gal. 3:12)**. When we simply believe and confess what has already been provided through Christ, that's taking the advantage grace provides and that's faith.

A person who is living under the law and a person who lives under grace will have very similar actions of holiness, but those two people's motivations are complete opposites. Legalists focus their attention on what they must do, while people living by faith focus their attention on what Christ has already done for them. For instance, the scriptures teach us to confess with our mouths and believe with our hearts, and we will receive from God. The legalist thinks, *That means I can get God to heal me by confessing "by His stripes I am healed."* However, the person who understands God's grace will not confess the word to get healed. He or she will confess, "By His stripes I am healed" because that person really believes it has already been done. In other words, we do not confess God's Word so that it will happen. Rather, we confess it because it has already happened.

Analyzing our "mind-set" is the simplest way of discerning whether we are operating in true biblical faith or in a legalistic counterfeit. If the motive for our actions is to be accepted with God, that's legalism (religion). If we live wholly out of faith and gratefulness for what God has already done, that's grace (Christianity). Grow in grace! What do you want to see in your business life? Believe that God has already provided it for you by grace, confess it and receive it today.

To Change Your Performance, Change Your Thinking

The Bible teaches us that our thoughts are the determining factor that controls our actions.

Proverbs 23:7 says, "For as he thinketh in his heart, so is he." Romans 8:6 says, "For to be carnally minded is death; but to be spiritually minded is life and peace."

Notice that carnal-mindedness doesn't just tend toward death. It *is* death!

No one can consistently perform differently from the way he or she thinks; therefore, we cannot change our actions without changing our thinking. It's not just *what* we think about that needs changing; we must also change our thinking process. Our emotions are linked directly to how we think.

All people have a perception or image inside them of what they are like. This image is not necessarily based on facts but on feelings. One negative experience can distort a person's perception of him- or herself for a lifetime. For instance, some people who are beautiful may think of themselves as ugly or undesirable because of unkind words spoken to them when they were children. Some who achieve great success still see themselves as failures, and this can become a self-fulfilling prophecy.

To a degree, psychology has correctly diagnosed this problem. Psychologists use terminology such as "self-esteem" or "identity" in relating these truths. However, today's secular wisdom is totally inadequate to help a person change the inner self-image. First, most people shift the blame for bad self-esteem or poor self-image to someone else - it has become popular to blame others for every negative thing in our lives. People often say, "I came from a dysfunctional family" or "My problems came because I'm part of a minority group" or "It's that woman you gave me" **(Gen. 3:12).**

Other people are not our problem!

All of us have had negative experiences. The choice is ours to become either bitter or better as a result of them. For every person who can claim some dysfunctional behavior because of a traumatic experience in his or her life, there are others who have had similar or worse things happen to them, yet they overcame their circumstances. Why? Because problems do not dictate failure; we have a choice.

I call heaven and earth to record this day against you, that I have set before you life and death, blessing and cursing: therefore choose life, that both thou and thy seed may live (Deut. 30:19 KJV).

God Almighty gave us a choice. God doesn't make the choice for us, and Satan can't make it for us. We have the privilege and responsibility to choose blessing or cursing.

Placing the blame on others is denying the real problem, and it will prevent us from finding a solution. If other people are my problem, then I'm in trouble because God did not give me the ability to control other people. The devil will always send someone across my path who knows how to push my buttons. If the problem is within me, then there is hope because through Christ I can change. This is freedom. Regardless of what others do, I can prosper through Christ.

After the psychologists try to place the blame for your problems on someone else, they try to bolster your self-esteem by having you focus on the positive things in yourself and minimize the negative attributes. That's not what the Bible teaches. Jesus said:

For without me ye can do nothing (John 15:5 KJV).
Whosoever will come after me, let him deny himself, and take up his cross, and follow me (Mark 8:34 KJV).

Paul said:

But God has chosen the foolish things of the world to confound the wise; and God hath chosen the weak things of the world to confound the things which are mighty; and base things of the world, and things which are despised, hath God chosen, yea, and things which are not, to bring to naught things that are (1 Cor. 1:27–28 KJV).

The Bible teaches that there must be an end to self-esteem before true service can begin. Christians should not try to store up the feeble positive attributes of their personalities. That is like trying to stop the bleeding from an amputated arm with a bandage; it won't work for long.

Regardless of how successful or talented we are in ourselves, we will eventually fail. If nothing else, we will get older someday and will not be as productive as before. If our self-esteem is rooted in our accomplishments, then it will ultimately fail. All the security we have found in ourselves will then come crashing down around us.

The Christian should have Christ-esteem. The apostle Paul said this:

I am crucified with Christ: nevertheless I live; yet not I, but Christ liveth in me: and the life which I now live in the flesh I live by the faith of the Son of God, who loved me, and gave himself for me (Gal. 2:20 KJV).

The secret to victorious Christian living is not found in self-improvement but in self-denial so that Christ can live through us.

This does not mean that God wants us to have a bad self-image. It just depends on which self we are talking about. You see, every born-again believer has become a new person in Christ **(2 Cor. 5:17, Eph. 4:22–24).**

The "old" person is corrupt and at best incapable of living the Christian life. This is the self that most people try to patch up and feel good about.

Give it up! We have to die to this old-self life with all its good and bad and find a new identity in Christ.

The new person is exactly as Jesus is **(1 Cor. 6:17)**! That's right. We are totally brand-new people in Christ. We have everything that Jesus has in our spirits **(1 John 4:17)**. We have a totally new identity in Christ. Why, then, would we want to fix up our old selves instead of just living in our new selves?

If we let the new person dominate us, we'll walk in power and victory in every area of our lives.

How can you tell if your thoughts and emotions are coming from the new born-again self or the old carnal self? God's Word is the key. Jesus says:

The words that I speak unto you, they are spirit, and they are life (John 6:63 KJV).

Any thought or emotion that agrees with what God's Word says about you is from your new person. Any thought or emotion that violates God's Word is from your old person—or the devil.

If you are angry at someone and refuse to forgive, you're in the flesh (old person). Just repent and get back in the spirit (new person), where you have love, joy, and peace **(Gal. 5:22)**. If you are afraid, you're in the flesh, "for God hath not given us the spirit of fear; but of power, and of love, and of a sound mind" **(2 Tim. 1:7)**. Instead of going to God and asking Him to remove the fear, just step out of the flesh and into the spirit, where there is no fear **(1 John 4:18)**. Just say, "Fear, I reject you in Jesus's name." If you're born again, you already have the Holy Spirit living on the inside of you and this means you can do all things through Christ which strengthens you **(Phi 4:13)** and this includes starting a successful business without money and enjoy financial freedom.

Chapter Four

How to Fulfill God's Purpose in Your Life

The place to start is the realization that the Lord has a specific and unique plan for you. He had this plan in mind before you were even born.

My frame was not hidden from you when I was made in the secret place. When I was woven together in the depths of the earth, your eyes saw my unformed body.
All the days ordained for me were written in your book before one of them came to be (Ps. 139:15–16 NLT).

God had all of your days written out before you were born. You aren't a mistake going somewhere to happen. You haven't been placed on this earth by chance. God orchestrated where and when you were born, the parents He gave you even if you were a victim of rape, your personality, and everything else about you for a specific purpose.

However, you can't assume that God's will is automatically going to come to pass in your life. It won't. God's will doesn't always come to pass. Take salvation, for instance.

The Lord is not slack concerning his promise, as some men count slackness; but is longsuffering to us-ward, not willing that any should perish, but that all should come to repentance (2 Pet. 3:9 KJV).

It's clear from this scripture that God wants everyone to come to repentance and be saved, yet we know not everyone does. God also wants everyone healed, yet people still live with sickness in their bodies. Likewise, God wants everyone to find and walk in the purpose He has ordained for them, yet not everyone will. But that's not God's fault.

Once you realize that *you* are the one responsible for discovering God's will, the next step is to start seeking God for it. He's not hiding His will from you. But you're going to have to do some seeking to find it.

Jeremiah tells us how we need to seek God:

Then shall ye call upon me, and ye shall go and pray unto me, and I will hearken unto you.
And ye shall seek me, and find me, when ye shall search for me with all your heart (Jer. 29:12–13 KJV).

Notice that the emphasis is on seeking with all your heart. As long as you can live without knowing God's will for your life, you will. But when you seek with all your heart, you will find it **(Matt. 7:7)**.

Present your bodies a living sacrifice, holy, acceptable unto God, which is your reasonable service.
And be not conformed to this world: but be ye transformed by the renewing of your mind, that ye may prove what is that good, and acceptable, and perfect, will of God (Rom. 12:1–2 KJV).

One mistake people often make in seeking God's purpose is to assume that whatever they're good at naturally must be what God wants them to do. So if they're naturally good at public speaking, they figure God must have called them to a speaking ministry of some sort.

God's will may have nothing to do with your natural gifts. If you can do something yourself naturally, you wouldn't need God's empowerment. Sometimes people's talents may be an indication of what God's will is, but many people have gifts and talents they don't even know exist.

Paul said God had separated him from his mother's womb and called him by His grace **(Gal. 1:15)**. God purposed for Paul to be a minister of the gospel before he was ever born. He didn't look at Paul's talents once he grew up and then decide He could use him. His life had been predestined, just as yours is. So if you look at only what you're good at to determine your purpose, you may totally miss it.

Most people are not accomplishing what God has called them to do. They may be doing good works, but that doesn't necessarily mean they're walking in God's purpose for their lives. Not everything that is good is of God.

God's Perfect Will Is Worth Finding

Supernatural peace and joy come when you're in the center of His will. And God's blessing and anointing will always be on your work when you're doing what He's called you to do.

Do you feel dissatisfied or unsettled with your life? Are you tired of just going to work, coming home, watching television, going to bed, and then getting up and doing it all over again? If so, it may be God who has placed this dissatisfaction within you in hopes of provoking you to start seeking out His perfect will. Don't wait another day to begin the search for God's will in your life. Knowing God's will for your life is a very small part of following and fulfilling that will. That comes as a total shock to most people. Most people think, *God, just show me what You want me to do, and, praise God, I can take care of it from here.* But actually the scripture teaches a very different attitude. Once you know God's will for your life, the next step—and maybe even a more important step—is finding out how to follow and fulfill His will.

In our society today, a lot people believe that the end justifies the means. As long as they get from here to there, it doesn't matter how they do it. That kind of logic has led to people making compromises. They'll do all kinds of things—operate in dishonesty, stab other people in the back, and do just about *anything*—as long as they feel they're fulfilling God's will. People often take a word from God, make a paragraph out of it, and put themselves out there in self-will. Or, like Moses, they take the Word and try to make it happen without asking God about the timing. *There is a right way and a wrong way to accomplish things. There is God's way, and there is a selfish way.*

It's not enough just to know that God has called you and that He has put an anointing on your life; you need to develop the character and the maturity to accurately represent Him. How you get from point A to point B is as important as knowing God's will for your life.

There is a way which seemeth right unto a man, but the end thereof are the ways of death. (Prov. 14:12 KJV).

Preparation Time Is Never Wasted Time!

I hope you're really getting this. For you to know what God wants you to do is wonderful, and that's powerful. It's a great privilege to have God reveal His will to you. I'm not diminishing that. But that is just the beginning step. It's like opening the door. You have not arrived. You are not complete. It is every bit as important to understand *how* to follow His will for your life as it is to know *what* His will is.

This is where the battle is: right between your ears! It's not what happens out there. Nothing external can defeat you. I know that's a statement many people wouldn't agree with. They think, "You don't understand. I've got this financial problem. I've got this relationship problem. I've got this business problem. I have to give up. I don't have any choice." But you *always* have a choice to believe God! Really, what defeats you is how you *think* about those things. You have to control your thinking! That's where it starts.

Everybody wants the testimony, but nobody wants the test! You can quit when things get hard, and most people wouldn't disapprove. They'd say something only if you *didn't* act that way. They'd get mad at you when you started saying you can overcome every situation. They believe you should be preparing for the worst.

The reason you have to look to Jesus is because it's in *your mind* that you faint. If you've started to follow God's will, but now you've come up against something that looks impossible, it's all in the way you think that will determine whether you experience victory or whether you quit. Are you going to be overcome by these circumstances? Are you going to let them defeat and discourage you? None of these things can destroy you unless you get weary and faint in your mind.

If you're in a bad situation and it's beating you, make sure not to faint in your mind! The way you think is causing you to be overcome by those situations. If you would think correctly, you would overcome!

You've got to get to where you look to Jesus and consider Him more than what you see in the mirror or feel in your body, more than what other people have to say to you—more than anything! You have to get to where God's Word impacts you more than anybody else's word!

Look at Joshua 1:8–9 (KJV):

This book of the law shall not depart out of thy mouth, but thou shalt meditate therein day and night, that thou mayest observe to do according to all that is written therein.
When you have observed the Word of God, when you have kept it before your eyes, when you meditate on it day and night,
Then thou shalt make thy way prosperous, and then thou shalt have good success.
Have not I commanded thee? Be strong and of a good courage; be not afraid, neither be thou dismayed: for the Lord thy God is with thee whithersoever thou goest.

You have to keep yourself encouraged because you will not fulfill God's will with a defeatist attitude. You will have to resist discouragement. You have to overcome obstacles that have been put in your path. I'm telling you, it takes effort.

Endure hardness, as a good soldier of Jesus Christ (2 Tim. 2:3 KJV).

If you're going to endure over the long haul, you're going to have to toughen up. Good soldiers don't indulge their feelings; they just do what they need to do. You're going to have to get to where you don't let things bother you. I know this flies in the face of how society thinks today: "Well, you just aren't in touch with your feelings. You're in denial." I don't deny that problems exist, but I do deny that any of these things can conquer me. I am absolutely in denial that I'm going to fail! God has called me to win! God has called me to be an overcomer! I can guarantee I will overcome anything that the devil forms against me **(Isa. 54:17)**. I am not in denial that sometimes things bother me, but I am not going to let them control me.

I tell you, if you are going to fulfill God's will, you're going to have to adopt these attitudes I'm talking about. You need to realize that **"better is the end of a thing than the beginning thereof" (Eccles. 7:8)**. It's wonderful to find God's will and move in that direction, but really it's only *after* you finish your course with joy that you realize all the benefits. This is what I'm trying to do—to share with you how you can fulfill God's will for your life. You can fulfill God's will in your life by knowing that God is always with you.

There is a statement that says, "Life is a series of choices." To some, this sounds simple, but it is true. Your decisions determine your destiny. You make decisions every day that move you closer to your God-ordained destiny—or away from it. There is no such thing as just sitting still or putting God's plan for your life on hold. That's a deception. God's will for you is intermingled with His will for others, and that is constant and dynamic. It's like catching a flight. You can miss it.

When you are on a road trip, those who are ahead of you can be valuable sources of information. It doesn't matter how you feel about them personally. The fact that they have already driven the road gives them insight that you need. They can tell you what accommodations and restaurants are available. Or they can let you know of a wreck or construction ahead and then advise an alternate route. You would be foolish not to draw on the insight of others who have gone before you. Every one of us has a

God-ordained destiny that is designed to touch the lives of others positively. Are you certain that the decisions you are making every day are the ones the Lord wants you to make? If you can't answer that affirmatively, then what is stopping you? Most people don't intentionally decide to miss their destinies; they just get busy with the cares of this life, and before they know it, they are in a rut that they can't seem to get out of.

But remember, your life is the result of choices—*your* choices. Others can influence or hinder you, but your choices are the determining factor of your destiny. It is never too late to make the right choices.

Studying God's Word will have the single most influential impact on your decisions and in your life. God's Word is a light to our path **(Ps. 119:105)**. All we really have to do is put the seed of God's Word in our hearts, and it will change us effortlessly. That's how God's Word works. Decisions do determine destiny, but those decisions must be based on the truth of God's Word.

Note that God's will for your life will always have to do with changing the lives of those in your world (sphere of contact) for the better. It will always have to do with winning for others. It will always have to do with loving others more than you love yourself because God is the one taking care of you. It does not have to take your entire lifetime to fulfill God's will and purpose for your life. However, the earlier you discover it, the better for you. Remember John the Baptist? His ministry lasted only about six months, yet he fulfilled his ministry. Jesus's ministry lasted about three years, yet He fulfilled His ministry. I believe that presenting this book to you is part of God's will for me because this book is going to change lives for the better all around the world. In your business life, ensure that you put other people first. That is part of God's will for your life. Ensure that people see Jesus on the inside of you because of the way you conduct your business and give glory to God. Some will even come to know Him through your attitude in business. This is part of God's will and purpose for your life. And then God will keep blessing the works of your hands. This is a sure way to be successful in business.

Chapter Five

The True Nature of God Is for You to Be Wealthy

Religion has taught us that prosperity is a dirty word used by people who are spiritually immature and selfish. That isn't true. Being blessed isn't about our will or what we want; it's about God's nature.

If you surveyed Christians today about what gives God pleasure, most would answer with something about repentance from sin. Probably not one out of a hundred would answer, "Seeing God's children prosper." On the other hand, if you asked one hundred parents what gave them pleasure, most answers would include something about seeing their children happy and doing well. If it is a parent's nature to want to see his or her children prospering and in good health, why would God be different?

Beloved, I wish above all things that thou mayest prosper and be in health, even as thy soul prospereth (3 John 1:2 KJV).

That's exactly the point Jesus was making in **Matthew 7:11.**

If ye then, being evil, knowing how to give good gifts unto your children, how much more your father which is in Heaven give good things to them that ask him? (KJV)

It is your father's good pleasure to give you the Kingdom. God doesn't just want you to have a cup; He wants you to have a cup that is overflowing.

God doesn't just want you to catch a few fish; He wants you to catch so many fish that your nets are breaking and your boat is about to sink.

Then He said,

> **"Throw out your net on the right-hand side of the boat, and you'll get plenty of fish!" So they did, and they couldn't draw in the net because there were so many fish in it (John 21:6 NLT).**

He wants everyone to have their fish with twelve baskets left over.

> **They all ate as much as they wanted, and they picked up twelve baskets of leftovers.**
> **About five thousand men have eaten from those five loaves, in addition to all the women and children! (Matt. 14:20–21 NLT).**

Many argue that the existence of struggling Christians is proof that it's not always God's will to see His children healthy and prospering. People say such things because they do not know the true nature of God. We live in a fallen world. We still have an enemy who wants to steal, kill, and destroy us. But that's why we must receive our blessing through a supply channel called faith.

> **But without faith it is impossible to please God; for He that cometh to God must believe that he is, and that he is the rewarder of them that diligently seek him (Heb. 11:6 KJV).**

God wants you to come to Him with the expectation of reward, not because of anything good you've done but because of His nature – He loves you unconditionally. I know this is the opposite of what religion has taught us, but He clearly illustrated this in the parable often referred to as the Prodigal Son. When most of us read this story, we relate with the son who ran away. We know our sin has made us unworthy to be in the presence of our Father. So maybe if we beg for forgiveness and confess our sins, God will let us live in His kingdom as a lowly servant. However, Jesus was telling this story not to illustrate man's nature; He was illustrating God's nature. Here is the story of the man who had two sons:

> **The younger one told his father, "I want my share of your estate now, instead of waiting until you die." So his father agreed to divide his wealth between his sons.**
>
> **A few days later, this younger son packed all his belongings and took a trip to a distant land, and there he wasted all his money on wild living.**
>
> **About the time his money ran out, a great famine swept over the land, and he began to starve.**
>
> **He persuaded a local farmer to hire him to feed his pigs.**
>
> **The boy became so hungry that even the pods he was feeding the pigs looked good to him. But no one gave him anything.**
>
> **When he finally came to his senses, he said to himself, At home even the hired men have food enough to spare, and here I am, dying of hunger.**
>
> **I will go home to my father and say, "Father, I have sinned against both Heaven and you. And I am no longer worthy of being called your son. Please take me on as a hired man."**
>
> **So he returned home to his father. And while he was still a long distance away, his father saw him coming. Filled with love and compassion, he ran to his son, embraced him, and kissed him.**
>
> **His son said to him, "Father, I have sinned against both heaven and you, and I am no longer worthy of being called your son."**
>
> **But his father said to the servants, "Quick! Bring the finest robe in the house and put it on him. Get a ring for his finger, and sandals for his feet. And kill the calf we have been fattening in the pen. We must celebrate with a feast. For this son**

of mine was dead, but now he is found!" So the party began (Luke 15:11–24, NLT)

Luke 15:20 explains how God feels about a sinner. He has love and compassion toward the sinner and is willing and ready, waiting for him to repent. When he was yet a great way off, the prodigal son's father saw him and had compassion, ran and fell on his neck, and kissed him. The son confessed his unworthiness to the father, but the father didn't even acknowledge it. There was no putting his son on probation or making him work his way back into the father's good graces. The father wasn't interested in punishing the son; he was too excited about getting back to what brought him pleasure: blessing his children.

He immediately restored his son into the family by putting a ring on his finger and shoes on his feet and dressing him in the best robe. Then he threw a party. The son's disloyalty and rebellion would no longer be remembered or brought up. It didn't matter anymore. So the true nature of God is to see us happy and prosperous, not to punish us. However, we must realize that sin has consequences. Whenever we disobey God, we simply open the door for the devil to come into our lives to steal, kill, and destroy us. We always have a choice to make.

God created man in His image, after His likeness. Then God said, "Let us make people in our image, to be like ourselves. They will be masters over all the fish in the sea, the birds in the sky, and all the livestock, wild animals, and small animals" (Gen. 1:26 NLT).

God made humanity to be His child, to live in beauty and abundance. There was no sickness, no death, and no lack. Humanity ruling over a perfect, blessed world was God's perfect idea. Imagine, then, how this loving Father must have felt when one day His children were running from Him. He had literally given them the whole world. There was only one thing that was bad for them: the fruit from the tree of the knowledge of good and evil. God had warned His children that they would die if they ate it, but they did not trust Him. Instead, Satan convinced them that God was holding out on them. They still believed there was some sort of enjoyment their Father did not want them to have. Lack of trust in God is still a major reason for sin today. This act of disobedience transferred humanity's authority over the earth to Satan, making the devil the "prince of this world."

The time of judgment for the world has come; when the prince of this world will be cast out (John 12:31 NLT).

It's also the reason there is poverty, lack, sickness, and death. These things do not exist in God's kingdom. They were not in the Garden of Eden. They are not in heaven, either. They exist only where Satan is in authority. When people blame God for poverty, suffering, and death, it's because they do not know the nature of God.

God hates human suffering. It was never His will. The world was created by the integrity of His Word. The Lord had given Adam the authority to rule over this world. Adam voluntarily chose to hand it over to Satan and separated himself from God. But God showed His loving nature. He could have said, "You made your bed. Now lie in it." He could have destroyed Satan's kingdom immediately, sending humanity to hell right along with him. But God didn't do any of that. He never stopped loving His kids. Instead of punishing them, He sent Jesus with the sole aim of paying for their sin with His death.

For even I, the Son of Man, came here not to be served but to serve others, and to give my life as a ransom for many (Matt. 20:28 NLT).

This made the way for the right relationship with God. Anyone who believes in the name of Jesus can be reborn as a child of God. The moment we receive this salvation, we are no longer sinners in His eyes but are righteous and truly holy.

> **You must display a new nature because you are a new person, created in Lord's likeness—righteous, holy, and true (Eph. 4:24 NLT).**

It's our nature to want to tell God how unworthy we are, but God doesn't see us that way.

> **I will never again remember their sins and lawless deeds (Heb. 10:17 NLT).**

As born-again believers, we are not trying to work our way back into God's kingdom. The moment we accept Jesus as our Savior, we are delivered from Satan's kingdom and translated back into God's kingdom.

> **For He has rescued us, from the one who rules in the Kingdom of darkness, and He has brought us into the Kingdom of His dear son (Col. 1:13 NLT).**

That's why Jesus taught His disciples not to worry about life or about having enough food to eat or enough clothes to wear. There is no lack in God's kingdom. If you need something in life, don't look at yourself and your abilities; instead,

> **Seek ye the Kingdom of God, and all these things shall be added unto you. He will give you all you need from day to day if you make the kingdom of God your primary concern.**
> **So don't be afraid, little flock. For it gives your father great happiness to give you the Kingdom (Luke 12:31–32 NLT).**

As you can see, it gives your Father great happiness to give you the kingdom. God wants you to be successful in business. What is it that you need to start your business? Ask Him today in faith, and it will be yours in Jesus's name.

Chapter Six

The Gospel: The Power to Receive

Anything You Desire from God

The word "gospel" does not just mean good news, it means news that is nearly too good to be true. Today most Christians think the word "gospel" is just a word that identifies religious things. They relate preaching about the wrath of God and impending judgment as the Gospel, but it's not.

It's true that those who don't accept the sacrifice of Jesus will spend an eternity in hell, but that's not good news. That's certainly not news that is nearly too good to be true, which is the real meaning of the Gospel.

The Gospel is the good news that, despite our sins and the judgment we deserve, God has provided complete redemption for us. Even more specially, the word "gospel" describes the grace that enables us to receive this forgiveness.

If I told you I had a gift of a million dollars for you, that would be good news. That would be nearly-too-good-to-be-true news. But what if I put down difficult or impossible conditions as things you must do to receive that money? Then it would cease to be a gift. Performance would be required on your part, so you would actually be earning the money. All your joy over the "gift" would fade away as you despaired about meeting the criteria. You would probably be upset with me. It would be better to have never been offered the money than to have it dangled in front of you and then placed out of reach through impossible demands.

That's the way it is with salvation. Just saying that Jesus provided salvation for us is not truly the nearly-too-good-to-be-true news unless it is emphasized that all Jesus provided is available to us by grace. The grace of God is the heart of the Gospel.

In **Acts 20:24**, Paul said he was testifying to the Gospel of the grace of God. He said the same thing in **Galatians 1:6**:

> **I marvel that ye are so soon removed from him that called you into the grace of Christ unto another gospel.**

Paul equated the grace of God with the Gospel. Any statements about God or the salvation He provided, without highlighting the grace of God, are not the true Gospel.

Telling people they are going to hell if they don't repent is true, but it's not the Gospel. Even telling people that Jesus provided an escape is not the Gospel, if we tell them they have to live holy lives to obtain that salvation. Putting any conditions on what we have to do to acquire God's provision denies grace and therefore is not the Gospel.

These are radical statements. Most of the church world doesn't define the Gospel this way, but that's the way Paul defined it—that "the Gospel is the power of God unto salvation," the power that we need to get saved and obtain everything that Jesus provided for us in the Gospel. If we seem powerless to receive from God, it's because we don't have a full revelation of the true Gospel. It's likely that somebody somewhere is telling us we need to perform to receive from God.

Most people today have not heard the true Gospel. They have heard that there is a heaven to gain and a hell to shun. They've heard that sin separates us from God and that they have to be forgiven for their sins. They've even heard that Jesus died to forgive their sins. Most people are yet to hear that all that Jesus provided for us is a free gift, accessible only by faith.

Because of our faith, Christ has brought us into this place of highest privilege where we now stand and we confidently and joyfully look forward to sharing God's glory (Rom. 5:2 NLT).

People are told about the forgiveness of sins and the wrath that awaits all who reject the sacrifice of Jesus, but so much burden of personal holiness is placed on individuals to receive what Jesus provided that the true Gospel has been perverted with all these requirements. That's why Paul wrote the book of Galatians. The Galatians had received the Gospel and had been born again, but after being saved, they left grace and went back to trying to earn the blessings of God through their adherence to rules and regulations. This brought some of the harshest rebukes the apostle ever gave to anyone:

O foolish Galatians, who hath bewitched you, that ye should not obey the truth, before whose eyes Jesus Christ hath been evidently set forth, crucified among you? (Gal 3:1 KJV).

He also said this in **Galatians 5:4**:

Christ is become of no effect unto you, whosoever of you are justified by the law, ye are fallen from grace.

You might ask, "Are you saying we can live in sin because salvation is by God's grace?" I am glad you asked that question. Paul addressed that very same question many times in the book of Romans. You could even say that if that question never comes up, then the true Gospel that Paul preached hasn't been presented. Most of the Gospel messages being preached today never raise that question because they aren't preaching the true Gospel.

Of course Paul didn't advocate a life of sin. Holiness is a fruit, not a root, of salvation.

But now you are free from the power of sin and have become slaves of God. Now you do those things that lead to holiness and result in eternal life (Rom. 6:22 NLT).

Paul also told us:

For the grace of God has been revealed, bringing salvation to all people.
And we are instructed to turn from godless living and sinful pleasures. We should live in this evil world with self-control, right conduct, and devotion to God (Titus 2:11–12 NLT).

Grace teaches us to live holy lives. Our holiness is a response to God's grace. Grace cannot be earned, or it wouldn't be grace.

And if they are saved by God's kindness, then it is not by their good works. For in that case, God's wonderful kindness would not be what it really is—free and underserved (Rom. 11:6 NLT).

When we clearly see the grace God has extended to us, the love of God, for us, will abound in our lives. Grace doesn't give us a license to sin, but it actually frees us from sin.

For sin shall not have dominion over you: for ye are not under the law, but under grace (Rom. 6:14 KJV).

Grace breaks sin's dominion over us. The law, or a performance-based message, gives sin dominion over us. The Gospel is the power you need in your life to receive whatever you need from God, including supernatural business ideas. This power works in you when you know that God loves you unconditionally. Hence you're qualified to receive anything you desire from Him. The Gospel is simply the unconditional love of God for you. Take advantage of it today to receive whatever you need in your business life.

How to Receive God's Best

To receive God's best, you have to recognize that it's all about receiving what God has already done, not about getting God to do something He has yet to do. We don't need God to heal us because by His stripes, we *were* healed **(1 Pet. 2:24)**. That miraculous healing power is already inside us. We only need to see it. We don't need God to move; we need to believe what He has already done and learn how to receive it. We do this by simply acknowledging those things the scriptures tell us He has already done and keep thanking Him for them.

Everything in our fallen world naturally goes from good to bad. Things don't get better without effort. We have to seek to find, knock to get the door opened, and ask before we receive **(Matt. 7:7)**.

> **I know the thoughts that I think toward you, saith the Lord, thoughts of peace, and not of evil, to give you an expected end [hope and a future]. (Jer. 29:11 NLT, additional words mine).**

When the Lord spoke to Jeremiah to write these words, Israel was devastated. The city of Jerusalem had been destroyed, and Nebuchadnezzar had taken many people captive to Babylon. Thoughts of peace were probably the last thing on their minds.

But Jeremiah continued:

> **Then shall ye call upon me, and ye shall go and pray unto me, and I will hearken unto you. And ye shall seek me, and find me, when ye shall search for me with all your heart (Je. 29:12–13 NLT).**

The key is, we have to seek with *all* our hearts. That's the missing element when we ask and don't receive. We give up too easily instead of insisting on what we need. We need to insist on what we want and act our faith through. **The Bible says in Acts 19:20 "So mightly grew the word of God and prevailed."** We have to reach a point where we won't live with anything less than God's best. That's faith.

That attitude is missing in the lives of far too many Christians. The bar of expectations, even within the church, has been lowered with regard to healing, finances, and more. The point is that God has far more for all of us than we are experiencing. Never, ever think that anything is too good for you. It's that attitude that keeps one from receiving the best from God.

Christians ought to be walking in supernatural healing. They ought to have successful businesses and walk in financial prosperity. Most, however, are just sick and broke. You will never receive God's best until you become completely dissatisfied with second best—mediocrity.

One of these days, we are all going to stand before God. And when we do, we will know all things even as we are known (**1 Cor. 13:12**). In an instant, we are going to know what we could have had while on this earth. We will understand that the same power that raised Christ from the dead was resident within us all along (**Eph. 1:18–20**).

We will discover that we didn't have to be sick, that we didn't have to live broke, and that we didn't have to be depressed and discouraged. We will realize that love, joy, peace, long-suffering, gentleness, goodness, faith, meekness, and temperance were living inside us the whole time (**Gal. 5:22–23**).

We don't have to limp into heaven, crying, "Praise God, we made it." We can live a life of victory now. Jesus died to deliver us from this present evil world (**Gal. 1:4**), not just the one to come.

Moses lived under an inferior covenant compared to ours (**2 Cor. 3:7–11**). Jesus said that John the Baptist was greater than Moses, and the least New Testament saint is greater than John (**Matt. 11:11**). Therefore, if Moses was still strong at 120 years of age with good eyesight (**Deut. 34:7**), why would we settle for less?

Unless you're willing to stand and fight the fight of faith, you will be overcome by this evil world. If you don't stir yourself up, you will settle to the bottom. This evil world isn't going to encourage you toward God's best, and most Christians aren't, either. Only you can encourage yourself through the word of God.

Sadly, religion is one of the strongest weapons Satan has to discourage people from believing in God's best. Many churches believe that God doesn't perform miracles today or, worse, that God is the one who wills for our lives to be in such a mess to break us or teach us a lesson. He sovereignly controls everything. That is not true. I encourage you to begin receiving God's best today in every area of your life.

God Made You a Winner

God designed you for success. He made you to be a winner. This is true for every person, regardless of what has happened in the past. God has never destined anybody to be a failure.

> **For I know the thoughts that I think toward you, saith the Lord, thoughts of peace, and not of evil, to give you an expected end (Jer. 29:11 KJV).**

This verse says that God knows His thoughts toward you, and His desire is to give you an expected end. You can walk in victory like Moses. As just mentioned, he was 120 years old, and his eyesight wasn't dim nor his natural force abated **(Deut. 34:7)**. He actually climbed a mountain the day he went home to be with the Lord.

These things are in the Word, and God is no respecter of persons. What we have today is superior to what Moses had in the Old Testament. Our success is guaranteed. Now, I'm not saying success can always be achieved without a fight or without effort, but we were destined for great things.

> **His lord said unto him, well done, good and faithful servant; thou hast been faithful over a few things, I will make thee ruler over many things: enter thou into the joy of thy lord (Matt. 25:23 KJV).**

If we are good stewards of what God gives us, He'll increase our gifts and give us more.

Many people look amazing on the outside, but in their hearts, they're miserable; they don't have joy or peace, and they certainly don't have success. Understand this: there is nothing in this world that will minister to you or satisfy you more than knowing that you are in the direct center of God's will.

According to the grace of God which is given unto me, as a wise master builder, I have laid the foundation, and another buildeth thereon. But let every man take heed how he buildeth thereupon.

For other foundation can no man lay than that is laid, which is Jesus Christ.

Now if any man build upon this foundation gold, silver, precious stones, wood, hay, stubble;

Every man's work shall be made manifest: for the day shall declare it, because it shall be revealed by fire; and the fire shall try every man's work of what sort it is (1 Cor. 3:10–13 KJV).

This is describing how as we go through life, we are either building with gold, silver, and precious stones or with wood, hay, and stubble. It does not say that everybody is building with gold, silver, and precious stones or that everybody is building with wood, hay, and stubble. We have a choice. The sad fact is that many of us build things in our lives and accomplish things that aren't what God intended for us, and we count these things as success.

A lot of people think wood, hay, and stubble are referring to adultery, fornication, and drug addiction, but did you know that people have done things that would appear to be godly—started churches, been in a foreign mission field, and written worship music and books —but none of it was led by God?

It doesn't matter whether the end result is good or not. God wants you to do what He has called you to do, and He wants you to do it out of His ability. I think what some call "burnout" is just people doing good things in their own strength and power. God's never had anybody qualified working for Him yet, so stop relying on your own ability. He is the one that qualifies you and gives you His ability. If you don't trust in the Lord, you can't accomplish the things He's planned for you, and you won't be a godly success. In your business life, acknowledge God and he will take you to where you never imagined. In all thy ways acknowledge him, and he shall direct thy paths. (Ps. 3:6 KJV)

Chapter Seven

God's Unconditional Love for You: Your Guarantee for a Successful Life

God loves me right now, independent of my behavior. He is not waiting for me to get my act together before He can love me. It's an unconditional love, not based on my performance. Therefore, I am assured it will continue. God's love for us is based on His nature. *He is love.*

But anyone who does not love does not love God—For God is love. (1 John 4:8 NLT)

This is great news that every Christian needs to hear: we do not need to do anything to earn God's favor. People who think they need to do something to earn God's favor can never measure up because God's standard is perfection. Jesus has already done that for us, so God loves us because Jesus has paid the price. All we need to do is to trust Jesus (the Word of God), and God will be pleased with us.

The Gospel as it is presented today actually drives peoples away from God. Instead of telling people what Jesus has done for them, people are told what they must do for the Lord to accept them. God's love is unconditional. Many people are told that God's acceptance and favor are conditional, based on their performance or whether they measure up to God's standard. This is not what the Bible teaches; God's true nature and love have not been accurately portrayed in some places.

The only thing that God demands from us is faith in the atoning work of Jesus Christ. The result we get from doing this brings such a response of love from us that the rest of the Christian life is nothing but a response to what Jesus Christ has done for us, not an effort to get Christ to respond to us. This is great news!

The apostle Paul is the one who really brought this truth to light. Paul shocked the religious people of his day by proclaiming justification apart from performance. The religious leaders couldn't comprehend this. How could they control people if they couldn't demand performance in exchange for God's blessing?

Paul's answer to these questions was that people's love for God would compel them to live holier accidentally than they ever did on purpose. Love is a greater motivator than fear of punishment or rejection. However, the leaders of Paul's day and many religious leaders today have totally rejected this truth.

When we struggle to believe that God's promises to us will come to pass, that is unbelief. But the root of that unbelief is our lack of understanding of God's unconditional love for us.

For whom we place our faith in Christ Jesus, it makes no difference to God whether we are circumcised or not circumcised. What is important is faith expressing itself in love (Gal. 5:6 NLT).

Our confidence in God's unconditional love for us is the key that makes our faith work. Without God letting us know what love is, we don't know what love is. Human love is never reliable. At best it is not unconditional. It is our understanding of how much God loves us that makes all the difference.

Many of us try hard to believe God when we should be seeking a greater revelation of God's unconditional love for us. Then our faith would just naturally work.

So don't be afraid, little flock, for it gives your father great happiness to give you the kingdom (Luke 12:32 NLT).

Let them shout for joy and be glad, that favor my righteousness cause: yea, let them say continually, let the Lord be magnified which hath pleasure in the prosperity of his servant (Ps. 35:27 KJV).

Once you are able to comprehend the revelation of God's unconditional love for you, doubt, fear, and condemnation will disappear, and your supplies will gravitate toward you. It's that simple.

There is more than just a superficial knowledge that God loves us. In Ephesians Paul prayed that the Ephesians would get a greater revelation of God's love for them.

When I think of the wisdom and scope of God's plan, I fall to my knees and pray to the Father,
The creator of everything in heaven and on earth.
I pray that from his glorious unlimited resources he will give you mighty inner strength through his holy spirit.
And I pray that Christ will be more and more at home in your hearts as you trust in him. May your roots go down deep into the soil of God's marvelous love.
And may you have the power to understand as all God's people should, how wide, how long, how high, and how deep his love really is.
May you experience the love of Christ, though it is too great to understand fully. Then you will be made complete with all the fullness of life and power that come from God (Eph. 3:14–19 NLT).

Notice **in verse 18** that God's love isn't just one-dimensional. There is height, depth, length, and breadth to it. Many Christians see God's love only as they would see a painting: in one dimension. They have never seen the multidimensional reality of God's love.

In verse 19, Paul says that as we experience God's love, which is superior to mere *knowledge* of God's love, then we would be filled with all the fullness of God. What a revelation! Are you lacking in any area of your life? If so, you lack a revelation of God's unconditional love for you. Experiencing God's unconditional love equals fullness. A deep revelation of God's unconditional love for us is the most important thing we can receive.

There are many ways Satan tries to block the revelation of God's love for us. One of the most deadly ways is that he has deceived us into thinking that God's love for us is tied to our performance. We think we have to do something to earn God's love. Again, that is not what the Bible teaches.

In the natural world, you get what you deserve. Employers don't hire you based on their love for you; you have to perform. If you perform badly, you are punished or fired. The same thing is true in most relationships. However, the nearly-too-good-to-be true news of the Gospel is that we don't get what we deserve. We get what Jesus deserves, free of charge.

Religion is one of the biggest propagators of the lie about the conditional love of God. Many teach that God's love for us is conditional, based on our performance. If we pray, go to church, pay our tithes, give offerings, and so on, then the Lord loves us and answers our prayers, but if we fail, then the Lord won't answer our prayers. That's not true!

Don't get me wrong, praying, going to church, paying our tithes, and giving offerings have great benefits, but we do not do them so that God will love us and bless us. The truth is that He has already done that. The first reason why we do these things is to demonstrate our trust in God and His word. The second reason we do these things is as a response and thanksgiving to God's unconditional love for us and because He has already provided for us all that we need in the spiritual realm. We simply need to use our faith to draw them to us. When we do these things we demonstrate our faith in Him.

Greater love hath no man than this, that a man lay down his life for his friends (John 15:13 KJV).

God's love for us is unconditional. God doesn't love us because of some virtue we possess. He loves us because He chooses to love us. It's His nature.

So understanding that God loves you unconditionally is your guarantee to ask Him boldly and receive for yourself earth-shaking business ideas to change your world. Be rest assured that He will give them to you if you ask in faith. Trust that He has already done it.

Keeping the Ten Commandments Doesn't Affect God's Willingness to Love Us

Keeping the commandments doesn't affect God's willingness to love us, but it affects our awareness of how much He loves us. If we live in sin, our conscience becomes defiled, and it condemns us. It is not God condemning us, but our conscience.

> **For I will be merciful to their unrighteousness, and their sins and their iniquities will I remember no more (Heb. 8:12 KJV). And their sins and iniquities will I remember no more (Heb. 10:17 KJV).**
>
> **When Jesus had lifted up himself, and saw none but the woman, he said unto her, Woman, where are those thine accusers? Hath no man condemned thee? She said, No man, Lord. And Jesus said unto her, Neither do I condemn thee: go, and sin no more (John 8:10 KJV).**

God loves us unconditionally. John was speaking of this same thing in **1 John 3:20**, when he said, **"For if our heart condemn us, God is greater than our heart, and knoweth all things."** However, as far as this earthly life goes, our awareness of God's unconditional love is everything. Therefore, we must keep Satan from blinding us to the unconditional love of God.

The most effective way of doing this is to give no place to the devil through sin. John went on to say in **1 John 3:20**, "Beloved, if our heart condemn us not, then have we confidence toward God." Holiness is essential in keeping our hearts assured of the love of God **(1 John 3:19)**. It's the nature of a Christian to walk in the light and not darkness. When you are rightly informed of who you are and what you have in Christ, holiness just naturally flows out of you. That's your nature, which means it's not something you do—it's who you are.

Matthew 13:15 says this:

For this people's heart is waxed gross, and their ears are dull of hearing, and their eyes they have closed; lest at any time they should see with their eyes and hear with their ears, and should understand with their heart, and should be converted, and I should heal them.

The word "waxed" means "to become gradually more intense or to increase" and shows that this condition of the heart is not something we are born with or that strikes us suddenly. It has to be nurtured over a prolonged period of time. This is why we must not violate our conscience, even in small things. Guarding our conscience will keep us sensitive to God and will stop our hearts from becoming hardened. If we will stay faithful to God, even in small things, then we will be faithful in the more important things also.

The Reason for Holiness in the Life of the Believer

The reason for holiness in the life of the believer is that when we obey sin, we yield ourselves to Satan, the author of that sin. It's like opening the door of our lives to Satan, who comes to steal, kill, and destroy us **(John 10:10)**. Yielding to sin is yielding to a person: Satan.

God doesn't impute the sin to us.

To wit, that God was in Christ, reconciling the world unto himself, not imputing their trespasses unto them; and hath committed unto us the word of reconciliation (2 Cor. 5:19 KJV).

Satan is the one who imputes our sin to us.

And I heard a loud voice saying in heaven, Now is come salvation, and strength, and the kingdom of our God, and the power of his Christ: for the accuser of our brethren is cast down, which accused them before our God day and night (Rev. 12:10 KJV).

Without our cooperation, Satan cannot lead us to sin because he has no power. It is the power we give to him, by saying yes to him, that he uses against us to steal, kill, and destroy us. All we need to defeat Satan is revelation knowledge from God's Word of who we are, what we have, and what we can do in Christ Jesus.

You must know who you are. **Matthew 4 and Luke 4** record the temptation of Jesus in the wilderness. One of the most amazing aspects of those temptations was that Satan began two of the three temptations with the words, "If thou be the son of God." The real temptation here was Satan's attempt to get Jesus to doubt who He was. That's the same way he attacked Adam and Eve. The serpent told Eve that if she would eat the forbidden fruit, she would be like God **(Gen. 3:5)**. The truth was that she was already like God, but she didn't know it. The first Adam sinned because he didn't know who he really was. The second Adam, Jesus didn't sin because He did know who he was. Knowing your true identity in Christ is one of the greatest defenses you can possibly have against temptation.

The only thing Satan does and can do is to deceive. He does this by telling lies to us just to make us doubt God's Word, like he lied to Eve in the garden and deceived her. He also tried the same trick with Jesus, but failed.

Ye are of your father the devil, and the lusts of your father ye will do. He was a murderer from the beginning, and abode not in the truth because there is no truth in him. When he

speaketh a lie, he speaketh of his own: for he is a liar, and the father of it. Jn. 8:44 KJV).

Jesus made it very clear that all power has been given to him and none to Satan. So his only weapon is to lie to make you doubt what God has said concerning you.

And Jesus came and spake unto them, saying, All power is given unto me in heaven and earth (Matt. 28:18 KJV).

If Satan can make you doubt God's Word, he has gotten you because you are going to do without.

But let him ask in faith, nothing wavering. For he that wavereth is like a wave of the sea driven with the wind and tossed. For let not that man think that he shall receive any thing of the Lord. A double-minded man is unstable in all his ways (James 1:6–8 KJV).

Our actions release either the power of Satan or the power of God in us. Although God is not imputing our sins unto us, we cannot afford the luxury of sin, because it allows Satan to have access to us. When a Christian sins and allows the devil opportunity to produce death in his or her life, the way to stop it is to confess the sin. God, who is faithful and just, will forgive based on the forgiveness He has already granted us in our spirit man(**Col. 3:13**) and also make available the power to overcome the weakness causing that sin when we believe Him to do so. This removes Satan and his strongholds.

The sins of a Christian don't make him or her a sinner any more than the righteous acts of a sinner make him or her righteous. Sin is a very deadly thing that every Christian should avoid at all costs because it hurts us and others, but it does not determine our standing with the Lord. A person who is born again is not "in" the flesh, even though he or she may walk "after" the flesh.

What is the motive for living a separated (holy) life? We live a separated (holy) life because our nature has been changed. We were darkness; now we are light **(Eph. 5:8)**. Many people argue for holiness in an effort to obtain a relationship with God, forgetting that holiness is our nature because the Holy Spirit lives in us as believers. We need to live holy lives because of the relationship we already have. It's the nature of a Christian to walk in the light, not in darkness. If Christians were rightly informed of who they are and what they have in Christ, holiness would just naturally flow out of them. It's their nature. It's our nature. So take advantage of God's unconditional love for you and who you are in Christ to ask God for great ideas and abilities that will enable you change your world for the better. With God on your side you can start a successful business without money.

Chapter Eight

The Seed of God's Word: The Key to Effortless Change in Any Area of Your Life

A true revelation of God's Word is the single most important element of a victorious Christian life. The Word of God often refers to itself as a seed. To conceive and give birth to the miracles you need, you must first plant God's Word like a seed in your heart, conception cannot take place without first planting the seed.

> **And he said, So it is the kingdom of God, as if a man should cast seed into the ground,**
> **And should sleep, and rise night and day, and the seed should spring and grow up, he knoweth not how.**
> **For the earth bringeth forth fruit of himself, first the blade, then the ear, after that the full corn in the ear.**
> **But when the fruit is brought forth, immediately he putteth in the sickle, because the harvest has come (Mark 4:26–29 KJV).**

The seed is the Word of God **(verse 14)**, and the ground is our hearts **(verse 15)**.

God created our hearts to bring forth fruit when His Word is planted in them. Just as a seed has to remain in the ground over time to germinate, so the Word of God has to abide in us. The Lord used the comparison of His

Word to a law of nature that is unchangeable, not an institution of man. The reason is that you can cheat or manipulate nearly all systems that men have created. The legal system can be beaten, letting the guilty go free. Our educational system can be beaten, passing students who haven't really learned the material. But you can't change seedtime and harvest.

What if a farmer waited until he saw his neighbors reaping their crops before he sowed his crop? Regardless of how sincere he was, and regardless of his justification for not sowing his seed at the proper time, he would not reap a crop overnight. The law of seedtime and harvest cannot be violated.

This is why our Lord chooses to compare the way His Word works to a seed. There is a germination process of the Word of God in your life that takes time and can't be avoided. But remember that the Lord is never late.

If you abide in me, and my words abide in you, ye shall ask what ye will, and it shall be done unto you (John 15:7 KJV). What would happen if you planted a seed in your garden and then dug it up each morning to see if anything was happening?

It would die and never produce fruit. You have to have faith (trust God) that the seed is doing what God created it to do.

Some people put God's Word in their hearts for a day or two, but if they don't see fruit almost immediately, they dig up the seed through their words and actions and wonder why it didn't work. You have to leave it in the ground over time. Also, there are different stages of growth.

First the blade, then the ear, after that the full corn in the ear (Mark 4:28 KJV).

Many people are impatient, waiting to bypass the growth cycle and get the full ear right now, forgetting that God is never late.

God's Word has to be planted like a seed in our hearts. Just as a seed doesn't release its life until it is planted into the ground, God's Word will not set us free until we get it in our hearts. Having the Bible on our tables, in our hands, or in our heads is not sufficient. We have to let God's Word penetrate our hearts.

When you plant a seed, the fact that nothing is visible above ground doesn't mean the seed isn't growing. Again, if you dig it up every day to see if anything is happening, it will die. A farmer has to leave his seed in the ground and believe it's growing, even though he can't see it. Likewise, you have to have faith that the seed of God's Word will do what God designed it to do—produce fruit in its time. Many people "dig up" the Word by speaking directly against what it says or, simply put, speaking the opposite of what God's Word says about them. They will let natural circumstances override what God says.

But when we meditate on God's Word, we are undergoing effortless change! We may not see ourselves changing, but we are—just as that planted seed is growing and changing under the ground, even though the farmer can't see it! This principle applies in every area of our lives, including our businesses. We need to say what we want to see in our business in line with what God says and watch our words come to pass, creating effortless change in our businesses.

Effortless change may sound impossible to most people. Most people view change as one of the most traumatic experiences in life. But there is a way to change effortlessly. That is to take the seed of God's Word and sow it in our hearts. Then the Word of God will produce all the change we need in any area of our lives.

You will never see an apple tree labor to produce an apple. It takes time, but it is never late, and it comes effortlessly in due time. Likewise, it is the nature of all true born-again believers to be like Jesus. But it can't happen without planting the seed of God's Word in your heart.

Growth (success) means change. Have you ever seen a plant that's green and growing and not in a constant state of change? For the plant, it's effortless. It just grows, and the change is evident to everyone. Your life should be just like that—green, growing, changing, and evident to the world. The plant never resolves to do anything. It just grows and produces fruit because of what it is. The Word of God is the same. When planted, it just produces—effortlessly. The way to plant the word of God is to believe it in your heart, knowing that God cannot lie, and to speak it out with your mouth thereby agreeing with God.

If you are like a lot of Christians, you have probably tried to change many times, but you find it hard and frustrating. That is because you haven't been going about it in God's way. You substitute praying, fasting, giving, and your own effort for the seed of God's Word. Don't get me wrong, praying, fasting, and giving are like water and fertilizer to a seed. A seed needs those things, but it is the seed itself that has the miracle of life in it. The only effort needed on your part is to put God's Word in your heart and mouth, protect it, nurture it, and say it to yourself. Then God's Word will produce the change.

In nature, we recognize that we can't have a harvest without planting seeds, but in the spiritual realm, Christians try it all the time. Instead of going to the Word and meditating on the scriptures themselves, they run to someone who has spent time in the Word and ask them for help. It's an attempt to find a shortcut around the process of seedtime and harvest. Then if they don't see results, they get confused and offended.

God has done His part; He has given us the Word. The Lord doesn't give us money directly.

Always remember that it is the Lord Your God who gives you power to become rich, and he does it to fulfill the covenant he made with your ancestors (Deut. 8:18 NLT).

One powerful means to become rich is ideas. God gives you good ideas through His Word or any means He chooses. The source of the power is in His promises in the Word. As we plant those promises in our hearts, the truth in His Word germinates, and prosperity comes.

Healing and other promises of the Word work the same way. Numerous scriptures get the point across that God's Word, for instance, is health to all our flesh.

For they are life unto those that find them and health to all their flesh. (Prov. 4:22 KJV).

He sent his word, and healed them, and delivered them from their destructions. (Ps. 107:20 KJV).

Yes, people can get healed by God without planting God's Word in their heart. It can come through the prayers of others or through gifts of healing or miracles **(1 Cor. 12:9)**, but it is not God's best way. God's best way is to take the seed of His Word and plant it in our hearts, where it will naturally and effortlessly produce the changes we desire.

This law of seedtime and harvest operates in every area of our lives. If we will plant God's Word in our hearts and then allow the seed to germinate and the plant to grow to maturity, we will reap the fruit of a harvest. That is God's best way. It is very important that you know God's Word and that you plant the seed of His Word in your heart long before you need the fruit of the harvest. It could mean the difference between prosperity and poverty, or even life and death even in your business.

We Are Not Just Heirs; We Are Joint Heirs with Christ

It would be wonderful to inherit any amount of God's glory and power. But the idea that we share equally with the one who has inherited everything God is and has is beyond comprehension. This is an awesome blessing, but it also places a tremendous responsibility on us.

In the same way in which a check made out to two people cannot be cashed without the endorsement of both parties, so our joint heirship with Jesus cannot be taken advantage of without our cooperation. Unaware of this, many Christians are just trusting that the Lord will produce the benefits of salvation for them. They are acutely aware that they can do nothing without Him, but they don't realize that He will do nothing without us **(Eph. 3:20)**.

The idea that God will do exceedingly and abundantly above all that we ask or think, by Himself alone, is not true. He has power, but it is the use of His ability combined with the power that works in us. "No power working in us" means no power of God will come through us. Remember that this power works in us when we believe His Word and do not doubt.

The exceeding greatness of His power to believers is power that is internal, not external, within the believer. It is working according to the faith that we exercise in the indwelling Savior. It was this principle that the apostle Paul was stating when he declared, "I can do all things through Christ which strengtheneth me."

The way we place our endorsement on the check is to believe what God promised in His Word and act on it as if it were true without doubt. Every word of God is indeed true. Jesus has already signed His name to every promise in the Word. We aren't waiting for Him; He is waiting for us.

Remember, planting what the Word of God says (in any area you want to see change) in your heart and confessing it with your mouth, without doubt, is the number-one key to experiencing effortless change in any area of your life. This includes starting a successful business without money, because life is spiritual, and the spiritual controls the physical. Take advantage of this truth today in your business life.

Chapter Nine

You Have God's Creative Ability: Meditate on God's Word for Successful Ideas

Why does an artist paint, a musician play, or an author write? Because they are overflowing with ideas and must express them.

Creativity is the overflow of a full heart and mind. But sometimes we're empty or full of the wrong material. How can we be full of the beauty that will spill out in wonderful visions, sounds, words, movements, and products or services? By taking the time to fill up on what is beautiful and what is true, which is the Word of God, also known as the wisdom of God. We can't spend our time and energy on worthless pursuits and stay creative because creativity requires energy, too. And if we want our creativity (ideas) to express the wisdom of God, then we must always be "filling up" by meditating on God's Word.

Take time to know God. Take time to soak up His Word and all that is beautiful. Take time to think about God's Word. As your inner wells fill up, you can be sure that creativity will soon be flowing out of your life in productive ways.

Do Not Limit God with Your Thinking

As a man thinks in his heart, so he is (Prov. 4:23 KJV).

Moses sent spies into the Promised Land, where they found a land flowing with milk and honey. But there were giants in the land, and the spies were afraid to enter—therefore limiting God. This all took place after God had guaranteed them success.

If thou shalt say in thine heart, These nations are more than I; how can I dispossess them?
Thou shalt not be afraid of them: but shalt well remember what the Lord thy God did unto Pharaoh, and unto all Egypt…
But the Lord thy God shall deliver them unto thee, and shall destroy them with a mighty destruction, until they be destroyed (Deut. 7:17–18, 23 KJV).

God gave them a promise, but He was also saying to them that if they believed in their hearts that the nations were greater than they were, then He would not be able to dispossess them. They were the ones who would determine what God could do. That alone should be enough to silence the voices of those who believe God is absolutely sovereign.

Now unto him that is able to do exceeding abundantly above all that we ask or think, according to the power that worketh in us (Eph. 3:20 KJV).

The phrase "according to" does not mean in proportion to or to the degree of the power of God that is working in you. It actually means "if you do not doubt" because Mark 11:23 says this:

Whosoever shall say unto this mountain, Be thou removed, and be thou cast into the sea; and shall not doubt in his heart,

but shall believe that those things which he said shall come to pass; he shall have whatsoever he saith.

James 1:8 tells us, "A double-minded man is unstable in all his ways." So doubt is the major problem, and it is the opposite of faith.

God wants to move in your life. He wants to bring you into your Promised Land. He wants to do something in your life that will cause you to wake up every morning excited about the day and full of His joy and peace. But it's not up to Him whether it comes to pass—it's up to you. So the question is, do you see yourself as a successful businessperson? Do you see yourself starting a successful business without money? Or do you think it's impossible or think it's up to God alone? My dear friend, you have a part to play. You must see it as something possible before you can activate the power of God in you to accomplish it. God can do nothing for you if you say no to your dreams or if you have no dreams.

Keep thy heart with all diligence; for out of it are the issues of life (Prov. 4:23 KJV).

Thoughts are powerful; they can deliver to you a glorious life, or they can keep you on the sideline of life, **The Bible says, "As a man thinks in his heart, so he is" (Prov. 23:7)**. You're the character of your thoughts.

If you can let the Word of God dominate your thinking, it will give you the right mind-set for victory, success, and dominion, with visions of limitless possibilities. This includes starting a successful business without money.

And be not conformed to this world but be ye transformed by the renewing of your mind (Rom. 12:2 KJV).

When your thoughts are consistent with the provisions of God's Word, your life will be a reflection of God's glory, for the glory is in the Word of God. What do you see? What are your thoughts? Direct your mind to think the right thoughts. You're the one to choose the way your thoughts must go; you're the one to create your thoughts.

> **Whatsoever things are true, whatsoever things are honest, whatsoever things are just, whatsoever things are pure, whatsoever things are lovely, whatsoever things are of good report, think on these things (Phil. 4:8 NLT).**

Every great idea starts with thoughts.

> **Study this book of the law continually, meditate on it day and night so you may be sure to obey all that is written in it. Only then will you succeed (Josh. 1:8 NLT).**

You can make your way prosperous and have good success by meditating on the Word of God and observing what it says. Meditate on it day and night. This shows that it's your responsibility to meditate always. Prosperity comes through meditation on the right materials.

God's responsibility is to give you the materials for prosperity, success, and the good life, and He already did that through His Word.

You are made in the image of God. You have God's creative ability. Therefore, create your prosperous life using His material that He has made available to you, which is His Word.

> **Then God said, "Let us make people in our image, to be like ourselves. They will be masters over all life—the fish in the sea, the birds in the sky, and all the livestock, wild animals, and small animals" (Gen. 1:26 NLT).**
> **So God created people in his own image; God patterned them after himself. Male and female, he created them (Gen. 1:27 NLT).**

Remember, you were created in the likeness of God. This means you were made to function like Him. And how does God function? He functions by faith. Jesus said, "Have faith in God."

I assure you that you can say to this mountain, May God lift you up and throw you into the sea, and your command will be obeyed. All that's required is that you really believe and do not doubt in your heart.
I tell you, you can pray for anything, and if you believe that you've received it, it will be yours (Mark 11:22–24 NLT).

So God is the God of faith. He created the whole world through words. Faith simply speaks what it wants to see and believes it.

As you study the book of **Genesis, chapter 1**, you'll observe that before God spoke creation into existence, He first had moments of meditation. The Bible says the earth was without form and void, and darkness was upon the face of the waters. This proves that you can start your business with no money. God started with nothing, and you're made in His image and likeness, which means that you function like Him.

In the beginning, God created the heavens and the earth.
The earth was empty; a formless mass cloaked in darkness and the spirit of God was hovering over its surface.
Then God said, "Let there be light," and there was light (Gen. 1:1–3 NLT).

When the Bible says the spirit of God was hovering over its surface, that was meditation.

Remember that the material for the meditation is the Word of God because the spirit of God is the same as the Word of God. Afterward, God began to say, "Let there be light," and everything He said came into being. This is the same principle and power He's given you to create your prosperous and victorious life.

It's up to you to meditate on the Word of God. Think, talk, and say aloud to yourself whatever you want to see happen. You will receive great ideas, and you will see yourself prosper and deal excellently in life.

Your commands make me wiser than my enemies [competitors], for your commands are my constant guide.

Yes, I have more insight than my teachers, for I am always thinking on your decrees.
I am even wiser than my elders, for I have kept your commandments (Ps. 119:98–100 NLT, addition mine).

Meditating on God's Word gives you excellent ideas that will put you on top in your business and finances. As you meditate on God's Word, your mind-set is elevated to make accurate decisions and choices in your business dealings. Everything you do will turn out excellently. Thoughts are powerful; they can deliver to you a glorious life or keep you on the sideline of life.

Don't copy the behavior and customs of this world, but let God transform you into a new person by changing the way you think. Then you will know what God wants you to do, and you will know how good and pleasing and perfect his will really is. (Rom. 12:2 NLT).

If you let the Word of God dominate your thinking, it will give you the right mind-set of victory, success, and dominion, with visions of limitless possibilities in your business or work.

What do you see? What are your thoughts? Direct your mind to think the right thoughts. You are the one to choose the way your thoughts must go. You are the one to create your thoughts. Remember, excellent thoughts will give you excellent ideas.

How to Decide on the Idea to Pursue

Ask God's wisdom first in your decision making.

Show me the path where I should walk, O Lord; point out the right road for me to follow.
Lead me by your truth and teach me, for you are the God who saves me. All day long I put my hope in you (Ps. 25:4–5 NLT).

If you need wisdom—if you want to know what God wants you to do—ask him, and he will gladly tell you. He will not resent your asking.

But when you ask him, be sure that you really expect him to answer, for a doubtful mind is as unsettled as a wave of the sea that is driven and tossed by the wind.

People like that should not expect to receive anything from the Lord.

They can't make up their minds. They waver back and forth in everything they do (James 1:5–8 NLT).

Intelligent people are always open to new ideas. In fact, they look for them (Prov. 18:15 NLT).

Get all the advice and instructions you can, and be wise the rest of your life.

You can make many plans, but the Lord's purpose will prevail (Prov. 19:20–21 NLT).

Plans succeed through good counsel; don't go to war without the advice of others (Prov. 20:18 NLT).

A wise man is mightier than a strong man, and a man of knowledge is more powerful than a strong man,

So don't go to war [marketplace of life] without wise guidance; victory depends on having many counselors (Prov. 20:5–6 NLT, addition mine).

We live in an Internet age in which you can get any information you need from any part of the globe. So take advantage of it, but make sure you go to reputable sources for your information.

How Do I Know I've Made a Good Decision?

And now, dear friends, let me say one more thing as I close this letter. Fix your thoughts on what is true and honorable and right. Think about things that are pure and lovely and

admirable. Think about things that are excellent and worthy of praise (Phil. 4:8 NLT).
Solid food is for those who have trained themselves to recognize the difference between right and wrong, and then do what is right (Heb. 51:14 NLT).

You will make good decisions more consistently if you spend consistent time in God's Word and act on its principles. This will enable you come up with products and services that will help humanity. It's all about making life better for others. Improving the lives of others and making the world a better place than you met it. If you think along these lines you will always come up with excellent products or services that will eventually make you very successful in business.

It's God That Gives Skill and Special Abilities

God gave these four young men an unusual aptitude for learning the literature and science of the time. And God gave Daniel special ability in understanding the meanings of visions and dreams (Dan. 1:17 NLT).

The four young men mentioned in the above scripture are Daniel, Hananiah, Mishael, and Azariah.

In all matters requiring wisdom and balanced judgment, the king found the advice of these young men to be ten times better than that of all the magicians and enchanters in his entire kingdom (Dan. 1:20 NLT).

The Lord also said this to Moses:

Look, I have specifically chosen Bezalel son of Uri, grandson of Hur, of the tribe of Judah.

I have filled him with the Spirit of God, giving him great wisdom, intelligence, and skill in all kinds of crafts.

He is a master craftsman, expert in working with gold, silver, and bronze. He is skilled in engraving and mounting gemstones and in carving wood. He is a master at every craft!

And I have personally appointed Oholiab son of Ahisamach, of the tribe of Dan, to be his assistant. Moreover, I have given special skill to all the gifted craftsman so they can make all the things I have commanded you to make (Exod. 31:2–6 NLT).

And the Lord has given both him and Oholiab son of Ahisamach, of the tribe of Dan, the ability to teach their skills to others.

The Lord has given them special skills as engravers, designers, embroiderers in blue, purple, and scarlet thread on fine linen cloth, and weavers. They excel as craftsmen and as designers (Exod. 35:31–35 NLT).

Are you called to help others? Do it with all the strength and energy that God supplies.(1 Pet. 4:11 NLT).

As we can see in the above scriptures, it is God who gives skills and special abilities. Ask Him today and receive whatever idea you need to excel in life. If you do so, you will be very successful and help countless numbers of people in your business.

Chapter Ten

The Most Important Thing about Your Business Idea

Men and women of different ages, races, and educational and family backgrounds have taken ideas and turned them into wonderful businesses. It's not what they were or had to start with that made them a success, but rather their ability to see a gap in the market and to go about it with passion and determination. You don't have to be an inventor to be an entrepreneur; you just have to find a gap in the market.

To succeed as an entrepreneur does not require money, education, or family connections. All that is needed is a clear idea for a product or service that is needed in the market but not available. To see this gap is what gives you the passion, energy, and determination to start a successful business. Just like a lion that has seen its prey can hardly be stopped, it's hard to stop an entrepreneur who has seen a genuine need in the market and knows how to meet that need.

Their roaring shall be like a lion; they shall roar like young lions: yea, they shall roar, and lay hold of the prey, and shall carry it away safe, and none shall deliver it (Isa. 5:29 KJV). For thus hath the Lord spoken unto me, like as the lion and the young lion roaring on his prey, when a multitude of shepherds

is called forth against him, he will not be afraid of their voice, nor abase himself for the noise of them (Isa. 31:4 KJV).

Even though the above scriptures are good examples of what a strong faith should be like, they also give us good lessons on what the tenacity of a good entrepreneur should look like.

How to Get Good Business Ideas

Always look out for a gap in the market. When you see a gap, an idea will be born. Then you move ahead to fill that gap or provide the solution. But the solution must be one that people want solved, not the solution you think they need. Always walk backward, from the market (gap) to the idea. It's the market that will tell you what to do; you do not tell the market what to do. Listen to the market. Let the market tell you what to do and how to do it.

The dominant forces in the market are forces of greed and fear. People will go for what is good, what makes them happy, and what adds value to their lives or makes them get ahead. They are afraid of what hurts them, inconveniences them, or causes loss for them. To start a successful business without money, any ordinary idea will not work. To have an idea with an edge (bait) is to do something better than anyone else or someone else, to do something no one has yet done, or to do something new and exciting or something that solves an existing problem. This is what it means to differentiate oneself.

Your Business Idea Must Have an Edge

The most important thing about your business idea is that it must have an edge (bait). It's important to note that any common idea will not work. To get an idea with an edge is not rocket science. It simply means to see the need (gap) first and then move to fill it (the solution). Don't ever get a product or service first and then start looking for who will need it; it's the other way around. God is the one Who helps you come up with uncommon ideas. Most of the time, you don't need to reinvent the wheel, although you may need to modify a current solution in the market to make your idea uncommon. Always make sure you see the need first before anything else.

> **Can two people walk together without agreeing on the direction?**
> **Does a lion roar in a thicket without first finding a victim?**
> **Does a young lion growl in its den without first catching its prey?**
> **Does a bird ever get caught in a trap that has no bait? Does a trap ever spring shut when there's nothing there to catch? (Amos 3:3–5 NLT).**

What are the most enticing, exciting, and valuable benefits your customers will get when they use your products and services? How can your products and services solve problems or meet needs? What actual problem does your product solve? Who is your ideal client? When you know the answers to these questions, you will have success. If a lion and a bird cannot be motivated without benefits, people can do much better. The bottom line is, what is in it for the people? Is your product solving the problem they want solved?

Have you wondered how Yahoo!, Facebook, Google, and other social networks make their money? In a nutshell, advertising revenue. But how do they get there?

Although different companies and individuals advertise products and services on their websites, the main product they are offering is the people who visit the websites. It is the large number of visits that attracts companies and individuals to advertise on these websites. And why do many people visit these websites? Because there is something in it for them. The people who manage those sites will give you a free e-mail address, free information, or a free platform from which to interact with your family members, loved ones, and friends.

At the end of the day, the product they are selling to those who advertise on their websites is the people who subscribe to their free services (benefits or bait).

The key is this: for people to come to you, there must be a bait (benefits for the people). You need to know what solution people are looking for. What is it about your product or service that can move people and cause them to part with their money because of that thing?

If you cannot catch a bird without a trap, and if a trap cannot spring shut when there's nothing to catch, what makes you think people will come to you with their money if your product or service has no edge or benefit for them?

An edge or a bait is the key an entrepreneur needs to attract money to finance his or her business ideas. Any idea without an edge or bait will not work. Most times, the best place to start is with yourself. If the idea has worked for you, it will likely work for someone else.

That which is far off and exceeding deep, who can find it out? (Eccles. 7:24 KJV).

A business edge is sometimes hard to find. Always remember that the edge you have in any market is either the benefit your product or service is bringing to people or the pain your product or service is helping people avoid. It's all about people and what they like or dislike. It's the same fundamental principle that moves any market. You make money by offering something they like, or you make money by offering them something that protects them from pain—something they hate or dislike.

This is what will motivate them to go for your business ideas. All over the world, people are motivated by benefits, whereas they run away from pain or loss. So your product or service must give them something they like to embrace or go after, or it must protect them from something they hate or run away from.

Failure to verify this is the reason most business die after takeoff. The owners of such businesses are not solving the problems that people want solved or their products and services are overpriced.

Great ideas come from God. Again, ordinary ideas will not work. You need an idea with a difference. This means it must meet an existing need in the market. Ask God to help you find it.

> **And the Lord said unto Abraham, after that Lot was separated from him, lift up now thine eyes, and look from the place where thou art northward, and southward and eastward and westward.**
> **For all the land which thou seest, to thee will I give it and to thy seed forever (Gen. 13:14–15 KJV).**
> **And I will give thee the treasures of darkness, and hidden riches of secret places, that thou mayest know that I, the Lord, which call thee by thy name, am the God of Israel (Isa. 45:3 KJV).**

My dear friend, God loves you unconditionally. He is willing to give to you as far as your eyes can see. Glory to God! What is it that you want? Can you see it? It's yours in Jesus's name.

The question is, do you see what God sees for you? Success, prosperity, and abundance? Or do you see what the enemy is showing you—failure, lack, and want? Whose report about you do you believe?

> **Who hath believed our report? And to whom is the arm of the Lord revealed? (Isa. 53:1 KJV).**

God's report says you can start a successful business without money and enjoy financial freedom. "The arm of the Lord revealed" means God's saving power for you. God's saving power has already been made available for you because the Holy Spirit lives in you as a child of God. Take advantage of Him today, and go for earth-shaking business ideas. They are for you. This should be your everyday consciousness. Never think failure because it's the lie of the enemy. Reject it verbally in Jesus's name whenever such a thought comes to your mind.

How to Know if a Business Idea Will Work

If people are willing to pay for your idea, then you know that you have something that will work depending on how you handle it. Presale is a powerful strategy that helps you ensure there's real demand for your product or service and minimizes financial risk. Presale helps you reduce assumptions about whether people will buy your product or not and gets you moving forward with your business quickly.

This is a much better solution than spending a lot of money and time and energy building a product, website, fancy logo, letterhead, business cards, and advertisements and paying to get legal protection for your product. People often become paralyzed by trying to get legal protection. It costs so much money to patent something. It's not the most important thing to do at the early stage. The most important thing to do is to know if there is anyone out there who will buy and use your product. So what you need to do to know if your business idea will work is rush your product to the market to build your customer base.

The big companies will not, most likely, be interested in your product until it has sold millions. If you have enough people who know about your product and are satisfied with it, then your business idea will work, and the money will naturally follow. This is the major turning point for any entrepreneur who wants to be successful. It's what makes the difference between those who fail and those who succeed.

It can seem impossible to sell your business idea and then turn it into a product or service after you confirm it would work, but it's exactly what I did with my business. I'm a procurement consultant. I started my business with no money. I had only an idea. I put my idea up as a proposal and presented it to the company I wanted to serve. The company is a multinational company. I had already seen a gap in that market, so I went ahead to presell my idea to them.

They gave me feedback (specifications they wanted) on my idea, which I then used to modify my idea to suit their purpose. After that, I presented them with a sample of the product. They approved it and offered me a contract. So I was able to presell my idea before moving on with the business idea.

This is the most important skill needed to start a successful business without money. It's called validating your business idea before starting it. This powerful principle always works whether you're selling a product or a service. Always let the people you want to serve confirm to you that they will pay for your product or service before you move on with the business idea.

The Bible puts it this way:

Can two people walk together without agreeing on the direction? Amos 3:3 (NLT)

It's a Bible-based principle, and it works. Once you can be sure that people will pay for your product, it's a confirmation that you're into a business that will likely work. It's at this point that you can look for sponsors because now you have something that works and the market is willing to pay for. People like to be part of something that will bring in money. This was what I did. I used the purchase order (contract document) I received from the company I wanted to serve to look for sponsors. I got a sponsor and gave him a copy of the contract document, which he used to confirm the genuineness of the transaction. Then he sponsored me. I had to part with a percentage of the business, but I moved forward.

Today I'm still servicing the company, and my business is doing very well. If this principle worked for me, it will also work for you. As you can see, my business needed money at some point, but I did not have money when I started the business. If your business idea is strong, it will always attract sponsors or investors, provided you don't give up looking for investors.

GOD ALREADY MADE MONEY AVAILABLE FOR YOUR BUSINESS

You will need money at some point in your business, but you do not need money to start. When you were born into this world, you were not born with money in your hands, but God knew you would need money someday to start your business. He already made it available before you ever needed money to start your business. You only need to see it and have faith (trust Him), and He will send the right idea or person along your path when you are ready for it. Just ask Him and receive by faith.

Acts 10:5 says, "And now send men to Joppa, and call for one Simon, whose surname is Peter: he lodgeth with one Simon a tanner, whose house is by the seaside: he shall tell thee what thou oughtest to do."

You know the gap you've seen in the market is strong if you are able to give people what they want and not give them something they don't want. At this point, just like the lion after its prey, you cannot be stopped unless you choose to stop yourself. Note that a genuine gap in any market is like a seed. It has the ability to attract investors if it is presented well to them. Always remember that once you see a gap in the market, it gives birth to an idea of what to do. It's the existing gap in the market that helps your idea work.

The question is this: what are you bringing to the table? If it's something that solves people's problems, they will naturally pay for it. You do not need money to start a business. You only need to solve a problem or provide a solution.

"But," you might ask, "what if the product needs to be built with money?" Look for people who can sponsor the product, and demonstrate to them how it works. Show them how it will solve the problem in question. They will want to be part of something that works. Don't take "no" for an answer and give up. Keep trying until you get a yes. You may have to give up a percentage of the business or profits, but always remember that 100 percent of a venture that doesn't go forward is zero. Do not let the fear of partnering with someone and giving up some percentage of your business idea cause you to lose the entire business.

> **There is hope only for the living, for as they say, "It is better to be a live dog than a dead lion!" (Eccles. 9:4 NLT).**

The market can withstand almost anything, but one thing it cannot withstand is a solution that people need. This solution should be your edge in the market you want to participate in. This is exactly what you are bringing to the table that will benefit people. If your bait or edge is good enough, you will surely attract buyers and sponsors. You don't have to have your own money to start a successful business.

The Storehouse Principle-A Way to Raise Funds to Start a Successful Business from Scratch.

What if you are not able to attract sponsors despite your best efforts? You simply need to have a job and start saving money from what you earn. The storehouse principle is one of the best ways to save money to start a business and look for investors or sponsors later. All you need is a job and time. The only thing you cannot afford is to give up.

One of the most neglected principles that God teaches is the storehouse principle.

> **"Bring ye all the tithes into the storehouse, that there may be meat in mine house, and prove me now herewith, saith the LORD of hosts, if I will not open you the windows of heaven, that there shall not be room enough to receive it." Malachi 3:10 (KJV)**
>
> **"My suggestion is that you find the wisest man in Egypt and put him in charge of administering a nationwide farm program. Let Pharaoh appoint officials over the land and let them collect one-fifth of all the crops during the good seven years.**

Have them gather all the food and grain of these good years into the royal storehouses and store it away so that there will be food in the cities. That way there will be enough to eat when the seven years of famine come. Otherwise disaster will surely strike the land, and all the people will die." Genesis 41:33–36 (NLT)

"Go to the ant, thou sluggard; consider her ways, and be wise: Which having no guide, overseer, or ruler, Provideth her meat in the summer, and gathereth her food in the harvest." Proverbs 6:6–8 (KJV) The ants gather their food into their storehouse. **Deuteronomy 28:8 says: "The LORD shall command the blessing upon thee in thy storehouses, and in all that thou settest thine hand unto; and he shall bless thee in the land which the LORD thy God giveth thee."**

God has a storehouse. He said we should pay tithes (10 percent) into His storehouse. He instructed Egypt to have a storehouse. Ants also have a storehouse, and so we definitely need a storehouse as well. God commands a blessing on our storehouses or savings. However, most people don't have a savings. This means they do not save money from what they earn; therefore, they are missing the blessing that God commands on our store house as Deuteronomy 28:8 tells us. The principle taught in the Word of God for our finances is as follows: pay God, pay yourself, and then pay everyone else.

Most Christians have learned to give (pay God), and they most certainly pay everyone else, but very few pay themselves. God wants to bless your savings. Begin the discipline of saving money regularly, and give God something to bless. **God can only bless what you have; He cannot bless what you need.**

You must save at least 10 percent of your monthly income, no matter how big or how little you earn. You might say, "I earn so little; therefore, I cannot save. The money I earn is not enough for me." Please understand that a lot of people earning much more money than you do are also not saving. The reason is that human wants are insatiable. This means that your needs will always expand to take all your income if you do not make a conscious effort to save at least 10 percent of your income. This is why a lot of people work for years and have nothing to show for all their labor, even when they earn a lot of money. They are not in control of their spending. Remember that you are the one who must be in control of your life. You must never spend more than 90 percent of what you earn. All your needs, wants, and problems must be contained within 90 percent of your income; otherwise, you are not in control of your finances because you're not putting anything aside for the future. The Bible puts it this way: **"A person without self-control is like a house with its doors and windows knocked out." Proverbs 25:28 (MSG)**

In other words, there is no security. If you can put aside 10 percent or more of your monthly income for some years, it will begin to make a lot of sense to you. Before long, the 10 percent will grow into a sizeable amount of money, which you can then use to make more money, provided you use it wisely by making only informed investments. Making an informed investment—like buying a secured piece of land in an upcoming but not very expensive area—will always be worth its weight in gold. Such an investment, if allowed to mature, may provide enough money to start a successful business for an entrepreneur.

Both the spiritual and practical must be working together for you to experience true abundance and financial freedom.

Chapter Eleven

The Most Essential Skill Needed to Start a Successful Business without Money

The most essential skill needed to start a successful business without money is validating your business idea. The greatest mistake an entrepreneur can make is failing to take time to know whether or not a market truly exists for his or her product or service before going into the business.

As an entrepreneur, you must recognize the fact that many others may be launching or working on similar products at the same time. You must check out the competition and make sure a niche (gap) exists in the market for your product or service. This is true whether you are building a product or importing one from abroad. The fact that a product is selling in the marketplace does not mean you will sell yours if you bring the same product into that market. A product may be trending, yet there may be no gap in the market for you if you bring in the same product. There may need to be a scarcity in the market, or you may need to create your own customer base before you can sell that product. Before anything else, make sure there is an existing demand (gap) for your product. Again, always go to the people you want to serve and see if your product is solving a problem they want solved. This is called validation of your idea. Failure to do this is one of the major reasons why businesses fail with money, energy, and time wasted, sometimes with terrible consequences for the business owner.

Validating your business idea is a Bible-based principle.

Again I say unto you, that if two of you shall agree on earth as touching anything that they ask, it shall be done for them of my father which is in heaven (Matt. 18:19 NLT).

Note that agreement is the key message here. In the marketplace, if your product is not solving a problem people are interested in, nobody will agree with you. So always get an agreement on your product or service first.

Can two people walk together without agreeing on the direction? (Amos 3:3 NLT)

Once again, the answer is no. Two people cannot walk together unless they agree. Agreement is a must. This proves that validation is necessary—the market agreeing with your product is the right way to go. You should never build something or import something into the market and hope someone buys it. Instead, you should validate your idea first to know if there is demand for it in the market. It is always better to give a sample of what you have to offer to the market to see if anyone is willing to pay for your idea.

Validating your idea will help you know how important your solution is to your customers. Your idea can turn into a profitable business only if someone is willing to pay for it. By the time you take this step, you will have successfully validated an idea and started a business.

The difference between an amateur and a professional entrepreneur is that the professional entrepreneur tries to validate his or her business idea before spending money or trying to build anything that will cost money, time, and energy. Validating your business idea before trying to spend money on anything will save you pain and wasted time. The reason is that validating your idea before starting a business minimizes your risk.

Until you validate your business idea, it is not time to register your company; buy business cards, do letterhead, get office space, pay for advertisements, hire workers; build a website; or secure legal protection for your product or service. These are added distractions you don't need while your business is still learning how to fly on its own. You must avoid these common business mistakes and focus on what really matters—getting customers who are willing to pay for your idea.

Always verify if you have what it takes to finish successfully, which is to find out what someone wants and is willing to pay for. This seems obvious in retrospect, but not many people think to do this before starting a business.

For which of you, intending to build a tower, sitteth not down first, and counteth the cost, whether he hath sufficient to finish it? (Luke 14:28 KJV).
Does a lion roar in a thicket without first fending a victim? Does a young lion growl in its den without first catching its prey? (Amos 3:4 NLT).

The reason you must validate your business ideas or presell it to the people you want to serve is that the money you want to make is in people's pockets. So you either pull the people to you with your idea, or you go to where the people are with your idea. Note that there is no market without the people. If a lion will not make a move until it first finds a victim (benefit), what makes you think anyone will pay for your idea or product without first seeing the benefits? Anything you can do to convince people to pay for your product or service will give you money through those people.

Feedback: The Real Value You Want from Your Customers

Prove all things, hold fast that which is good (1 Thess. 5:21 KJV).

Once you find potential customers through validation of your idea, they will give you feedback, and that is the real value you want. Listen to the ideas of people who are willing to pay for your product or service.

The business dictionary defines feedback as follows: "The process in which the effect or output of an action is 'returned' (feedback) to modify the next action." Feedback is essential to the working and survival of all regulatory mechanisms found throughout living and nonliving nature, and in man-made systems such as educational systems and the economy.

As a two-way flow, feedback is inherent to all interactions, whether human to human, human to machine, or machine to human. In an organizational context, feedback is the information sent to an entity (individual or a group) about its prior behavior so that the entity may adjust its current and future behavior to achieve the desired result. Feedback occurs when an environment reacts to an action or behavior. For example, customer feedback is the buyer's reaction to a firm's products and policies, and operational feedback is the internally generated information on a firm's performance. Response to a stimulus (such as criticism or praise) is considered feedback only if it brings about a change in the recipient's behavior.

As you can see, feedback is a vital tool for any entrepreneur. Take full advantage of it to improve on your business idea.

Feedback Is a Bible-Based Principle

> **Moses gave the men these instructions as he sent them out to explore the land: "Go north through the Negev into the hill country.**
> **"See what the land is like, and find out whether the people living there are strong or weak, few, or many.**
> **"See what kind of land they live in. Is it good or bad? Do their towns have walls, or are they open camps?**
> **"Is the soil fertile or poor? Are there many trees? Do your best to bring back samples of the crops you see." (It happened to be the season for harvesting the first ripe grapes.)**
> **So they went up and explored the land from the wilderness of Zin as far as Rehob, near Lebo-hamath (Num. 13:17–21 NLT).**

Notice that when Moses sent the twelve spies out, what he wanted was simply feedback. It's a Bible-based principle, and it works. This is why you must validate your business idea or product. Take it to the marketplace to get feedback. The aim of the feedback is to improve and win, not to get discouraged and back down. Feedback helps you win because it helps you see what and where to improve your product or service. Also, Moses told the spies to enter the land boldly. So boldness is required. Never take your product or service to the market fearfully. Fear is never part of the solution. Note also that timing is part of the equation. The spies went during the season for harvesting the first ripe grapes. This shows that they went early in the season of grapes. So in presenting your product to the people you want to serve, you need to get the timing right. Use your knowledge of the market and ask the Holy Spirit to help you in this area.

There is a time for everything, a season for every activity under heaven (Eccles. 3:1 NLT).
And Moses sent to spy out Jaazer, and they took the village thereof, and drove out the Amorites that were there (Num. 21:32 KJV).

We see this principle once again. Moses used this strategy again and again for victory. Feedback helps you win. Just as Moses drove out the Amorites, feedback can help you capture your market share and drive out your competitors or even crush the competition.

And Joshua the son of Nun sent out of Shittim two men to spy secretly, saying, Go view the land, even Jericho. And they went, and came into an harlot's house, named Rahab, and lodged there (Josh. 2:1 KJV).

Joshua also used this principle for victory. That product or service you have in your hand is the spy you need to spy on the market secretly and bring feedback to you. So you have to send it boldly into the marketplace to do its job and get for you the much needed feedback.

> **And the children of Dan sent of their family five men from their coasts, men of valor, from Zorah, and from Eshtaol to spy out the land, and to search it, and they said unto them, Go, search the land: who when they came to mount Ephraim, to the house of Micah, they lodged there (Judg. 18:2 KJV).**

Notice that they sent men of valor. This means boldness or determination in taking on great danger, especially in battle. So when you have a product or service you believe will fill a need or a gap in the market, you must be bold about it. Don't let fear stop you. Boldly take it to the market (the people you want to serve), and get valuable feedback on it.

Notice also that most of the time, the spies will lodge at a place as a base. This shows that getting feedback could take a while. Do not be in a hurry if you want a good result. Let it take as long as it needs to take to get good feedback. This may require repeated visitations to the marketplace.

> **Then answered the five men that went to spy out the country of Laish, and said unto their brethren, Do ye know that there is in these house an ephod, and teraphim, and a graven image, and a molten image? Now therefore consider what ye have to do (Judg. 18:14 KJV).**

Feedback will help you get information to know what to do and win in the marketplace of life. It helps you focus on what is important. Find out what the problems are, identify a solution, and validate it. It helps you to overdeliver with execution. So always go where the customers are, and show them how your product solves their problems. Get feedback from them, and use it to improve your product or service. Do not focus on solutions without first knowing what the problems are. It is always better to work backward (via feedback) from the needs of your potential customers, starting with yourself.

How to Convince People to Sponsor Your Business Idea or Buy Your Products

After you have validated your business idea, it is wise to look for an expert who can work with you to put together a good business plan. This is one of the best choices you can make while in the preliminary stages of your business because a quality business plan will make it easier for you to get potential investors for your business idea. To attract investors into your business, you need to know the worth of your business and be able to communicate it convincingly to prospects. This will surely attract investors.

You must realize that the power to start a successful business without money is within you, not with anyone else. Everything you need for a victorious life is within you. That's the way God made you. Let's assume that getting the capital to establish the business you want has been a challenge. Don't wait for anyone to bring the money to you! The most important thing is not the capital you need for the business but what you can see in your heart. Can you see a successful business? Or are you thinking that without first seeing the capital in your hands, you cannot have a successful business? That is the lie of the enemy from the pit of hell. **Deuteronomy 7:17 says**, **"If thou shalt say in thine heart these nations are more than I; how can I dispossess them?"**

My dear friend, did you know that this was in your Bible? That God is waiting on you to make up your mind on what you want Him to do for you as much as you are waiting on Him to do something for you? Yes, God can do all things, but He will do nothing without your cooperation. The reason is because you are not a puppet or a pawn on a chess board that can be pushed up and down at any time; rather, you have the ability and the authority to choose, and God will always respect that because He loves you unconditionally. What an awesome God we serve. God is asking you the same question today: "If you say in your heart that without capital you cannot start a successful business, how, then, can I help you?"

Jesus said unto him, if thou canst believe, all things are possible to him that believeth (that it is possible) (Mark 9:23 KJV, addition mine.)

The Bible did not say all things are possible to the person who has capital. My dear friend, when you were born, you were not born with capital in your hands, yet God knew you may need to start a business someday. This means that He provided all you will need for your business before you were born into this world. All you need to do is to believe in His wonderful plan for your life, which includes capital for your business, and receive it from Him. Just say to yourself, "I'm unstoppable. Money cannot limit me. I receive the capital I need for my business (mention the amount) in Jesus's name." Whether you believe it or not, it works because there is a God, but it works for those who believe in the divine provision of the almighty God.

Remember that God also started with nothing, He created everything with words and you were made in His image and likeness. This means that you were made to function like Him.

If you hold on to the picture of the business, you don't have to worry about how the capital will navigate to you or who God would use to make it happen. Understand that anything and everything that's consistent with life and godliness has already been given to you; it's all in your spirit! **The Bible says, "Through faith we understand that the worlds were framed by the Word of God, so that things which are seen were not made of things which do appear" (Heb. 11:3).**

Ephesians 1:3 says, "Blessed be the God and Father of our Lord Jesus Christ, who hath blessed us with all spiritual blessings in heavenly places in Christ."

If God has blessed you with all spiritual blessings in the heavenly realms, it means that you already have all good things that exist in the spirit realm; they are in your spirit. Therefore, you can call forth capital from within you. Halleluiah! Remember, it's what you say that will eventually happen, not what your flesh (what you see, feel, hear, etc.) is telling you. Your spirit is a reservoir of good things; you can bring forth anything you want from within you through what you say and God will bring it to pass through anyone or means He chooses.

Seest thou a man diligent in his business? He shall stand before kings; he shall not stand before mean men (Prov. 22:29 KJV). Be thou diligent to know the state of thy flocks, and look well to thy herds (Prov. 27:23 KJV)

What the Bible is simply saying is that you should be on top of your game. If you're not convinced about your business idea, it's likely that no one else will be. To attract investors into your business, you need to know the worth of your business and be able to communicate this convincingly to prospects. This will surely attract investors.

The challenge of convincing people that your product will work before they buy it can be solved with videos and testimonials. When it comes to all businesses (large and small), the success of the business depends heavily on word of mouth. Testimonials are formal forms of expression that support that concept. Testimonials strengthen the credibility of you and your business, and, as you know, people will not do business with you if they don't trust you and find you to be credible.

It is written in your law, that the testimony of two men is true (John 8:17 KJV).

One of the main reasons people don't buy what you are selling is lack of trust. Your product or service can be astounding, but if prospects don't trust you, they won't buy. On the other hand, if you are able to show testimonials from clients who believe in what you do and how you do it, other people will want to try you and your offerings out as well. It is an excellent idea to gather as many testimonials as possible.

Remember, testimonials from others have a powerful impact on your business. You are the only person who cannot give a testimonial for your own business.

Whenever you have a positive interaction with a business associate and he or she expresses an interest in any of your business offerings, it is a good opportunity to ask that person for a testimonial. If you have given someone a product, ask him or her for an opinion on the product, and if it is positive, subsequently ask that person for a testimonial. It is great if you are able to obtain both written and video testimonials. Both media are effective and work in different ways. Video touches people visually and emotionally, and written testimonials touch people emotionally and mentally. It is also good from a convenience perspective: many people prefer either written or video testimonials, depending on how busy they are and how important convenience is to them.

> **Doth not the ear try words? And the mouth taste his meat? (Job 12:11 KJV).**
> **O taste and see that the Lord is good; blessed is the man that trusteth in Him (Ps. 34:8 KJV).**

Note that your product will never be perfect. Focus on finding people who want it, and then you can evolve your product to be better over time. Think about the first-generation cars compared to today's cars.

Pricing Your Product as Low as Possible Is a Bible-Based Principle

As a business starter, make it easier for people to say yes to your product or service by pricing it as low as possible.

> **Do not despise these small beginnings, for the Lord rejoices to see the work begin, to see the plumb line in Zerubabel's hand … (Zach. 4:10 NLT).**
> **There is a way which seemeth right unto a man, but the end thereof are the ways of death (Prov. 14:12 KJV).**

Better is the end of a thing than the beginning thereof: and the patient in spirit is better than the proud in spirit (Eccles. 7:8 KJV).

Price your product in such a way that you will achieve your aim, which is to make a sale.

A faithful man shall abound with blessings, but he that maketh haste to be rich shall not be innocent (Prov. 28:20 KJV).

Be aware that even when the market accepts your product, the market changes every day, because it is made up of people who are fickle. So your expectations for how much you intend to make from your product may not be consistent at the beginning. The profit will definitely come with time if your product truly solves a problem that people want solved. Never try to force the market. So trying to achieve unrealistic goals is setting yourself up for failure before the product picks up momentum.

If you believe that your product has an edge (competitive advantage) in the market, the money will naturally come.

A little one shall become a thousand, and a small one a strong nation. I the Lord will hasten it in his time (Isa. 60:22 KJV).

How to Overcome Fear of Failure When Starting a Business without Money

Always remember that fear and doubt are never part of the solution, but faith and courage are. Then remember that God has not given us the spirit of fear.

For God hath not given us the spirit of fear but of power and of love and of a sound mind (1 Tim. 1:7 KJV).

The New Living Translation puts it this way:

For God has not given us a spirit of fear and timidity but of power, love, and self-discipline.
Be strong and courageous! Do not be afraid of them. The Lord your God will go ahead of you. He will neither fail you nor forsake you (Deut. 31:6 NLT).

Fear is not good if it keeps us from doing the things we ought to do. We are not meant to live in fear. Fear may leave us unsettled, unsecure, and doubting. However, if you don't take a step of faith (action on your part), what you want won't happen. Courage doesn't always roar. Like someone rightly said - sometimes courage is the little voice at the end of the day that says, "I'll try again tomorrow."

Fear of failure is one of the issues people are most unwilling to talk about when starting a business. Get over your fear; it is holding you back from success. You must get away from the need for your product to be perfect. Starting from where you are is the key, provided you know that your product is solving a problem that people want solved. It's not really as hard or as uncomfortable as you think to overcome fear. All you need to do to overcome fear is to face it head on and say with a loud voice, "Fear, I reject you in the name of Jesus." It will surely give way.

What to Do When You Believe in the Efficacy of Your Product or Service, but No One Else Seems to See What You're Seeing

The simple answer is persistence and determination, provided you're sure that you have the needed solution.

Brethren, I count not myself to have apprehended but this one thing I do, forgetting those things which are behind, and reaching forth unto those things which are before (Phi. 3:13 KJV).
Persistence and determination alone are omnipotent. The slogan "press on" has solved and always will solve the problems of the human race (Calvin Coolidge).

Our society is so caught up in winning; we forget that most of the great men and women in history have, at one time or another, failed at something often repeatedly, and discouragingly. But each failure is nothing more than a brick in the wall that forms the foundation of our success. We can't forget that (Calton Young).

A person who removes a mountain begins by carrying away small stones (Chinese proverb).

In the book *The Power of Resilience,* Dr Robert Brooks and Sam Goldstein said, **"Failure should be our feedback, not our undertaker. Failure is delay, not defeat. It is a temporary detour, not a dead end."**

Failure is something we can avoid only by saying nothing or doing nothing. It may motivate you more toward your own goals to know that some of the most famous and well-known people in modern times had to overcome obstacles as difficult as any other person before they finally reached the top. But with the Holy Spirit in us we can get it right the first time if we ask him to help us.

Thomas Edison's father called him a "dunce." Edison's headmaster in school told him he would never make a success of anything.

Henry Ford barely made it through high school. The media asked Joe Paterno, former head coach of the Penn State University football team, how he felt when his team lost a game. He replied that losing was probably good for the team since that was how the players learned what they were doing wrong.

Setbacks and failures mean little or nothing in themselves. The whole meaning of any setback—or any success, for that matter—is in how we take it and what we make of it.

We often look at high achievers and assume they made it without much effort. Usually the opposite is true, and the so-called superstar or "overnight success" most likely had an incredibly rough time before he or she attained any lasting success.

You may not know the background of a certain laundry worker who earned sixty dollars a week at his job but had the burning desire to be a writer. His wife worked nights while he spent nights and weekends typing manuscripts to send to publishers and agents.

Each one was rejected with a form letter that gave him no assurance that his manuscript had even been read. But finally a warm, more personal rejection letter came in the mail to the laundry worker, stating that although his work was not good enough at this point to warrant publishing, he had promise as a writer, and he should keep writing.

He forwarded two more manuscripts to the same friendly (yet rejecting) publisher over the next eighteen months, and as before, both were rejected. Finances got so tight for the young couple that they had to disconnect their telephone to pay for medicine for their baby.

Feeling totally discouraged, he threw his last manuscript into the garbage. His wife, totally committed to his life goals and believing in his talent, took the manuscript out of the trash and sent it to Doubleday, the publisher who had sent the friendly rejections. The book *Carrie* sold more than five million copies and, as a movie, became one of the top-grossing films in 1976. The laundry worker, of course, was Stephen King.

This story lets you know that you must never give up at the first sign of "no" to your idea or product. Believe in your product if you are sure it has benefits that people want.

Chapter Twelve

How Successful Entrepreneurs Did It

In Nigeria I read, in a gospel tract published by Faith Tabernacle Lagos-Nigeria, the testimony of Ignatius Okpojero, who in his own words said "I was tattered, battered and in fact things were terribly bad for me". He started his business with 75 Dollars which he used to buy shoe polish and brush. He began to polish peoples' shoes for a living. Through that he raised enough money to pay for tuition fee at a computer training school. When he graduated from the school there was no job. The Spirit of God told him to create a job for himself. So he gathered some people and started teaching them how to operate the computer. Today he has his own building and three cars. If he could make it in business, you too can make it. The principle is to look out for a human need and move to fill that need. In this instance the needs were shoe polishing and computer education.

In his book *How They Started—How Thirty Good Ideas Became Great Businesses* and also on his website (www.startups.co.uk), David Lester profiled many successful entrepreneurs in the United Kingdom. Here are some excerpts of testimonies of some of them regarding how they were able to turn their ideas into successful businesses based on the gap they saw in the marketplace of life.

They all had one thing in common: each one of them saw a gap in the market they intended to serve, which gave them an idea of what solution the market needed, and they were able to verify if the idea would work before investing money in it. They did not need money to start. They just had an idea that would work. Some of them became very successful without investor's funds. For others the idea attracted investment to their businesses. If this worked in the United Kingdom, it will work for you anywhere else in the world because it is based on a principle that works. That principle is to look for a human need first (gap in the market), and then move to fill that need. It's all about serving the people.

But he that is greatest among you shall be your servant (Matt. 23:13 KJV).

Pimlico Plumbers–Charlie Mullins

Charlie Mullins started his plumbing business at the age of twenty-seven in 1979. His company (Pimlico Plumbers) has a turnover of about £20 million per year. He turned the plumbing industry on its head, creating a reputable brand bursting with reliable, trustworthy plumbers. Charlie is Britain's first millionaire plumber and has differentiated his business enough that he has inspired a new generation of plumbing companies. Charlie had a working and in-depth knowledge of plumbing before he was ten years old. Since then, his whole working life has involved plumbing so when it came to going out on his own, he was in a position to note all the things customers disliked. The public was fed up with plumbers arriving late, canceling appointments, and turning up badly presented, all of which were perceived to be plumbing industry standards.

The Gap in the Market –Birth of the Idea

Charlie very simply did the complete opposite of what was perceived and used it as a simple yet highly effective way of distinguishing his business from other plumbers. He comments that you either improve your service or don't become a busy company. Arriving well presented, on time, and doing a good job are milestones in promoting a different image of the plumbing industry. Proud of his ambitious attitude, which he feels sets him apart from his contemporaries, Charlie took this working idea forward, making the most of opportunities when they arose. By using his common sense and making the most of opportunities, Charlie began to build his plumbing empire pipe by pipe.

Charlie left school with no qualifications and went straight into a four-year plumbing apprenticeship, following in the footsteps of his local plumber hero. After that, he began working for himself, built up a client base, and created a good reputation.

Validation of His Idea

In the early years of his business, to win jobs, Charlie insisted that no payment was made until the job was completed to the customer's absolute satisfaction. There were no investors, bank loans, or business strategies.

Success Story

The business was self-funding and expanded when Charlie had the money to do so. Its reputation was created by word of mouth—it takes a long time to spread. But eventually, once it gets moving, your reputation can get you somewhere before you get there, Charlie notes.

From the beginning, Charlie strived to offer a 24-7 service. Because he was the only plumber in the company this facility was not as guaranteed as it is today, but Charlie always tried to work to this policy. Over the years, Pimlico has endeavored to create a more reliable service than its competitors and now guarantees its twenty-four-hour availability and to have someone with the customer within the hour, if necessary.

Charlie is very much into the gradual. He allowed the business to grow organically. Without forcing anything and without ever having a rigid business plan, Pimlico Plumbers undoubtedly relied on the relentless need for plumbers, coupled with principles of reliability and integrity to generate and keep business. Today, almost 80 percent of Pimlico's workload is generated from people who have used the company before.

Charlie is vehement that Pimlico has never and will never have outside investors. He acknowledges that while the business could have been ten times bigger and probably national if he had taken on investors, it may not have been better. He does not want to lose control of the company. **As Pimlico established itself, Charlie did receive a number of offers of investment, but his concern was for Pimlico's reputation.** Reputation takes a long while to build up, yet you can lose it overnight. He says, "We are the company we are because we provide the service when people want the service."

From small beginnings to the company's present-day success, managing thousands of jobs a week, Charlie emphasizes the need to keep it simple. He has followed a lucid marketing campaign, which he believes is crucial for any business, combining advertisements with prominent premises signage and smart, well-maintained, and highly branded vehicles.

Glasses Direct–James Murray Wells

At twenty-two years old, James Murray Wells came from nowhere and took the world of optometry by storm. He started his company, Glasses Direct, in 2004 as a student. The spectacular success of his company led him to being named the "UK Startups Business of the Year" in 2005. He talks about how he did it and why the investors are queuing up around the block to get involved in his company.

The Gap in the Market–Birth of the Idea

James was studying at the West of England University in Bristol when he discovered he needed reading glasses.

So he visited his nearest high-street optician but was appalled when he found that his new metal frames, "essentially some wire and two pieces of glass," cost £150. "I was managing on a student loan, and £150 was a fortune—half a month's rent. I just couldn't understand why my glasses were so expensive, and my curiosity led me to investigate further." He began to call manufacturers, opticians, and industry insiders, but he was met with a "wall of silence."

Then a disgruntled employee at a laboratory in the north of England gave him the lowdown.

"He talked me through the industry," James says. "And it turned out that my £150 pair of glasses probably cost only about seven pounds to make."

James was supposed to be hammering the books in preparation for his finals but instead found himself immersed in the glasses industry.

He learned about optometric testing, how the frames are made, and how the lenses are cut.

He discovered that the market is around 70 percent controlled by major high-street retailers.

But, most significantly, he learned that he could make glasses for a fraction of the price that they were being sold on the high street.

Being only twenty-one and with no business background, most manufacturers were extremely reluctant to open an account with Glasses Direct. Nonetheless, after much hard work and a fair amount of rejection, James found a few manufacturers happy to work with him, and he agreed to terms with them.

Validation of the Idea

As a test to know if his business idea would work, James agreed to forward his own prescription to the manufacturers, who would then send him a pair of glasses with the correct lenses. The test worked. When the glasses arrived at his house a few weeks later at a cost of just £6, that was the moment, he says, when he first thought, *this will work.*

Murray Wells planned to focus his new business just on supplying glasses to people with prescriptions, unlike most opticians, who conduct eye tests for customers and then supply them with glasses or contact lenses afterward. He called it Glasses Direct to make it very clear what the business was about.

Success Story

James enlisted the help of some students at his university to build a website and design a logo.

He then used the final installment of his student loan and some money from his father to establish Glassesdirect.co.uk. They began trading in September 2004.

Manufacturers were initially reluctant to deal with him because they did not want to endanger their relationships with high-street opticians, but eventually they relented. In a year, Glasses Direct had sold 22,000 pairs of spectacles. James believes this saved UK consumers an estimated £2 million.

"People generally can't believe our Glasses Direct prices," he says, "as the high-street shops are maintaining retail prices at ten to twenty times the cost. What I'm giving people is choice, and they are delighted. An average pair of glasses is manufactured for less than seven pounds, so I charge just over double. Even with advertising and overhead, I still make a profit." His business has gone from strength to strength, and he now employs seventeen staff members. Turnover is around the £1 million mark.

"It's all been a bit of a whirlwind," he admits. "But I have always been determined to get very big, very fast."

To aid expansion, Glasses Direct is now seeking investment from venture capitalists. However, James says they are also seeking him.

"It's been a lot easier than I ever thought it would be," he says. **"We've literally been getting new calls from potential investors every day. It's wonderful, and we're in a very enviable position to choose who we want to work with."**

The big players in the optical industry appear to have accepted that Glassesdirect.co.uk is here to stay too—even if they're not happy about it.

James remains undeterred by the high street's desire to stamp him out, but is looking to shake off the David vs. Goliath tag.

Friends Reunited–Steve Pankhurst and Jason Porter

Friends Reunited is the immensely popular website that lets people make contact with old school friends. Since its launch in 1999, Friends Reunited has become one of the most popular websites on the Internet, attracting more than ten million members and a deluge of media coverage. The brand has now expanded to cover three sites, with the Pankhursts keen to establish their idea outside the United Kingdom.

Gap in the Market –Birth of the Idea

Steve Pankhurst developed the idea www.friendsreunited.co.uk when his pregnant wife, Julie, became very curious about whether any of her old school friends had children themselves.

Steve created one of the web's most successful sites from his bedroom in Barnet, north London. Steve and his business partner, Jason Porter, had worked together for about ten years and had been writing big Internet systems for insurance companies—this was at the height when people had loads of ideas for the Internet, about 1998–99. We felt that we had some good ideas, and we could do it much better than what was going on at the time.

Validation of the Idea

"We did check out the market. The way the idea came about was that we wanted to track down some friends when Julie was pregnant, so we went on the Internet and looked on some message boards. It was like searching for a needle in a haystack.

"Because we were both database programmers, we thought, *No, that's not the way you do it; you start off with your school and work that way.* To be perfectly honest, I didn't think it would work in Britain. I didn't think that school reunions would be taken in the same way as America, with their high school yearbooks and things like that.

"We came across a similar site in America, but we found out that it was just American and not UK schools, so that's when the money bells started to ring in my head! It amazes me now that a successful site in America hadn't been repeated around the world.

"We did it very quietly. We didn't do masses of advertising; we just relied on word of mouth and PR, which is completely free. It just seemed to tap into the imagination of people. By the summer of 2001, the media had picked up on it, and it created a kind of snowball effect, which was more like an avalanche.

"Jason and I had a lucrative contract for these insurance companies, but to be honest, we were bored essentially making money for other people. Friends Reunited was sitting there, and you could see the potential of it. It had a couple of mentions in the press, and by March 2001 it had twenty thousand people on it.

"You could see it working. People were getting reunited, and at this time it was costing us nothing apart from our time, which was every spare moment of the day, as we were working at the same time. But it wasn't making any money, either. The advertising revenue had bombed out on the Internet—it was make or break time.

"At this time, no one had any way of making money through websites, apart from advertising," Steve continues. "There were very few subscription-based services out there. So we decided to pack in our jobs and decided to go full time with this. At the same time, we introduced the five-pound charge—it's still free to register, but five pounds to contact people. At that time we had no idea whether it would work or not.

"We had a lot of complaints from people saying, 'How dare you charge? The Internet is free.' It wasn't until we wrote back and explained that actually it was costing us a couple of thousand pounds a month on servers, a thousand pounds a month on bandwidth, and we're spending all our time, two families, on this, and people don't realize. All we're trying to do is make a living. To be fair, most people accepted it."

Success Story
Steve Pankhurst and Jason Porter sold the company to ITV in 2005 for a reported £120 million.

JoJo Maman Bébé–Laura Tension

"It's often said that entrepreneurs have something to prove, and I think I fit that category," Laura Tension says. "I'm the youngest in my family, and most of my siblings were really academic, but I wasn't. I found school quite challenging, and I either respected the teacher and took to the subject, or I just couldn't see the point.

"One Christmas, we were given a project of making toys for children in Africa, and I loved it. I found I was good at sewing and designing, and while most of my school mates made just one toy, I made ten. I realized they were a commodity that could be sold. Suddenly, I didn't have to be the one who was always getting into trouble. I was actually really good at something. My parents bought me a sewing machine, which I still have, and I started making clothes for friends.

"I set up my first proper enterprise when I was still in my teens—a menswear business called Distinctive Silks. I later traveled to the Middle East and India to source the best materials. I went out for three months, but I ended up staying away for nearly two years.

"When I came home, I was determined to start a fashion company but decided to get some industry experience first. So I wrote to every British manufacturer/retailer I could think of. I was offered a job as a retail manager at Aquascutum and spent eighteen months with the company.

"At twenty-three, I tried to set up my own fashion company, but I couldn't get backing from the banks, which told me to get a private investor. I didn't want to give up control of my business, so I moved into property, spotting a gap in the market. I traveled around rural France to find suitable properties to let. I would find British clients by putting advertisements in the UK press. I ran this business for three years and sold it in 1992, making about fifty thousand pounds. It was enough to get started, and by then a bank was prepared to match my investment."

Gap in the Market –Birth of the Idea

Although Laura knew she wanted to set up some sort of clothing company, she says that she was still at that time unsure about what area she would be focusing on and was indeed quite open to ideas. The idea that became JoJo Maman Bébé came to her in a remarkable way. At Easter time in 1992, Laura was involved in such a bad car accident in France that she was flown by air ambulance back to the United Kingdom with two broken legs, crushed ribs, a shattered foot, and damage to her cheeks and jaw, confined to the hospital for a long rehabilitation process. Because the orthopedic ward she was due to stay on had no beds, Laura recounts how she was transferred to a cancer ward shortly after her arrival. It was there that she met the woman with whom she credits as providing the inspiration for Jojo Mama Bébé—the one-stop shop for all your maternity, baby, and nursery needs.

According to Laura, sometime during her recovery she began talking to the woman in the bed beside her and discovered that this woman, age thirty-two, was a mother to two young girls whom she wished to purchase some clothes for. She was upset, Laura recalls, because while she was too ill to leave the hospital, she could not find anything she considered nice in any of the mail-order catalogs. She complained to Laura that what was available was often limited and of poor quality.

Although Laura had no experience in the children's wear market and was not a mother herself, she recognized that this lady's comments might be just the fantastic business opportunity she was looking for. As a result, she describes how she plotted an early release from the hospital. Once she was out—despite still being in a wheelchair—she started work immediately.

The first thing she did was look into whether other young mothers had the same complaints her hospital neighbor had raised. Was this really a gap in the market? She concluded, of course, that there was a gap, and she set out to fill it.

Laura printed questionnaires and used a mailing list of people interested in children's wear for her research. This research taught Laura several key points about her chosen market. First, she noted that while people certainly wanted nice children's wear, what they predominantly wanted was maternity wear.

"I decided to launch via mail order, and there was a gap in the market for a fashionable collection for pregnant women that didn't look like maternity wear."

Validation of the Idea

Laura introduced the innovative idea of making a maternity version of the black business suit. In those days, she says, companies designing maternity wear tended to produce frumpy clothing such as tent dresses and dungarees and would always avoid black due to "mad superstitions" that wearing black might somehow cause a woman to miscarry. **But when Laura commissioned such items (a maternity version of the black suit), she found that various niche groups picked it up and that people responded well.** As a result, she says that part of creating a successful business is sticking your neck out and not being afraid to try something new.

Success Story

In JoJo Maman Bébé's first year, she sent out thirty thousand catalogs and sold clothes worth £50,000, a figure that increased fivefold in the following year to £250,000. This proved to be the inspiration for JoJo Maman Bébé, the £19 million turnover business that Laura founded.

S&A Foods–Perween Warsi

This company (named after Perween's sons, Sadiq and Abid) now has about 750 staff members and a turnover of about £65 million. It supplies major retailers in the United Kingdom and has expanded into Europe. "When I realized it was difficult to buy good-quality Indian food, I thought that maybe I could make a difference," she says.

The Gap in the Market –Birth of the Idea

S&A Foods was literally inspired by a samosa its founder bought from a supermarket in 1986. Appalled at its quality, Perween Warsi saw her chance to make a difference.

Perween's initial approach was direct. She simply prepared some of her own samosas and convinced a local Indian takeaway to try them. They sold well, and she began supplying the outlet regularly. Encouraged, she approached other takeaways and local delicatessens, while expanding her range. However, supplying to the local trade was never going to be enough. Her eye was always on the bigger prize: the big retailers.

Validation of the Idea

She began calling supermarkets, persisting until S&A was asked to take part in blind tasting sessions at Asda and Safeway. **Her food triumphed over more established food manufacturers, and she received an order.** There was, however, one problem.

"When Asda offered me the contract, they assumed S&A Foods was a full-fledged food-manufacturing business," she recalls. "At that time I was still making the dishes in my kitchen, so we had to build up the business quickly!"

So Warsi took a gamble. In 1987, S&A Foods joined the Hughes Food Group, with the resulting investment injection allowing them to open their first factory in Derby.

"Although at the time it was good for the business to join with Hughes, as it meant we could afford to build a new factory and create one hundred extra jobs, I wasn't in control of the direction the business was going," she says.

It would come at a cost later, but for now she could begin to fulfill her ambition of supplying supermarkets with her products, something she still does today.

"You need to have something different, unique, and better that they currently don't have to add value to their shelves," she says.

However, she warns against focusing too heavily on the client and forgetting the people who really buy the food—the customers. "Obviously, the whole of the supply chain is geared up to manage our customers' needs and requirements," she says.

"My belief is that my business should be tailored to meet the needs of my customers and my consumers, not food production."

She had hit the big time from nowhere, but her initial strategy was to come back to haunt her. In 1990, the Hughes Food Group went into receivership, leaving S&A's future looking bleak. **Perween had to fight for the survival of the business, and in the following year, with the support of venture capitalists 3i, she led a management buyout (MBO).**

Success Story

It was 2004 before Warsi regained 100 percent of S&A. In spite of this setback, the business performed well during the 1990s and is now expanding across Europe.

Alongside a passion for food, Perween believes strongly in staff development. S&A has an on-site learning center, where staff can gain work-related qualifications and learn languages.

Both are important to the success of S&A (twenty-three languages are spoken on S&A's factory floor), but Perween says it is about more than just work. "It inspires them to reach their potential," she says, "both in and out of the workplace."

Her role has changed considerably since starting up. She used to spend most of her time in the factory or seeing customers. Now she's more focused and has a "very capable management team" around her. However, she is still involved in S&A's day-to-day running. Her passion for food has not diminished, and she still spends time in India researching new flavors and tastes.

"It's important when you're developing new dishes to actually speak to people, see what they are eating, and see what new ideas are coming through," she says.

She won the Woman Entrepreneur of the World Award in 1996 and was given a seat on the Confederation of British Industry's National Committee in 2002.

Bebo–Michael Birch

How does $850 million for three years' work sound? The Birches, who sold social-networking site Bebo for that tidy sum, would probably suggest it's worth a few late nights in the office.

Like so many Internet success stories, that of husband and wife Michael and Xochi Birch initially appears to be an overnight sensation. The real story includes five preceding Internet startups and learning the valuable lesson of knowing when to let go.

Michael's love affair with online ventures began shortly after he quit his position at an insurance firm. "I was always entrepreneurial," he says. "But I was trying to be entrepreneurial in the wrong place for me - an insurance company, and it was probably the most frustrating thing in the world. Then the Internet happened, and I quickly realized this was the perfect medium."

When Michael married Xochi, a Californian, he promised they'd spend five years in England, five in the States, then decide where they wanted to settle. Having spent eight years in the United Kingdom, it was time for Michael to live up to his end of the bargain, and the couple relocated to San Francisco.

Michael insists his penchant for online startups would have developed even if he hadn't moved to the state that brought us Google, but he admits it's "not a bad place to be running an Internet business."

Settled amid a strong community of online developers, the Birches set to work on their own ventures. However, online success was not instant, and a few years of trial and error ensued.

The first two projects, a self-updating address book and a programmers' tool, fell by the wayside. Then came BirthdayAlarm.com, an e-card and diary alert tool that sends out reminders so you never miss a friend's birthday. The site was a major hit and is still going strong to this day, albeit without the Birches' direct involvement.

Having acquired a taste for dot-com success, Michael and Xochi turned their attention to online social networking and developed Ringo.com, which they sold a few months later. "We just didn't have the resources to throw at it. We'd had three offers in a week and it was hot property at the time."

Gap in the Market –Birth of the Idea

In early 2005, armed with cash from the Ringo sale and confident they had the skills to set up an even better social network, the Birches delivered Bebo to the online community. **Michael was aware he had to enter the market with a unique proposition. For him, it was to address the youth market with a product that matched their user demands and understood exactly what they did and also what they did not want from a network host. The second fundamental issue for Michael was to create an environment to harbor and encourage a network—something he insists is key to the member numbers Bebo attracted.** "It's about trying to encourage a healthy community without trying to dictate how that community behaves," he explains. It might sound like obvious stuff, but Michael insists it was these subtleties of product that made Bobo stand out from the crowd.

Validation of the Idea

Within a month, Bebo was generating revenue from advertising. It took another month for that money to come through, so within eight or nine weeks it was cash-flow positive. "Ultimately, we built something we thought we'd find useful and wanted to use, and we hoped enough people shared the same opinion," Birch says.

Success Story

Enough people did. Successfully tapping into the youth demographic, Bebo enjoyed phenomenal growth during the three years Michael and

Xochi were at the helm, topping forty million users, and ranked number one for social networks in several countries including, at one stage, the United Kingdom.

"Starting Bebo was a similar process to starting the other ventures," Michael says. "The difference was, this took off from a very early stage. I think that was because we'd gotten a lot better at learning how to do things. There wasn't so much trial and error. After a while, you start to get an instinct for what works and what doesn't."

The site's sole revenue model was advertising. However, Michael soon recognized the potential ads have for frustrating users. He refused to allow pop-ups or pop-unders and restricted ads to one unit per page.

"It's important to provide a service that works for the advertiser, but equally, it's in the advertiser's interest for users to embrace ads, not be frustrated by them." Time will tell if Bebo's new owners maintain this stance.

Chapter Thirteen

Practical Bible-Based Principles that Will Help You Minimize Mistakes and Realize Your Dream as an Entrepreneur

A real entrepreneur does not set out just to make plenty of money and become rich overnight. The reason for starting a business varies, from needing to earn a living after redundancy to wanting a certain quality of product or service which didn't previously exist, or even simply wanting to see if they could succeed within an exciting, fast-growing market. In addition to the passion and commitment needed to become successful in any business, you also need the ability to see a gap in the market and move ahead to fill it. It's the gap in the market that drives the entrepreneur, rather than the desire to get rich quickly. To work long hours, take risks, and make personal sacrifices requires a strong motivation that people who are in it just to make money cannot sustain. An entrepreneur is someone who is out to meet a need, to solve a problem, and by so doing improve lives and make the world a better place. He is out to make a difference. This is the driving force of a real entrepreneur, and as a result money follows naturally.

Listed below are Bible-based practical steps an entrepreneur can take to minimize mistakes and become successful.

Business Plan and Market Research

Research the market you're attempting to break into and see if you are bringing a solution the market needs. How will you make money? If you can't answer this question, you shouldn't start your own business. The purpose of any for-profit business is to make money. Before you embark on your business venture, you must have a detailed plan for how to do this and be able to answer the questions below. These are fairly fundamental and by no means exhaustive:

o   In what ways will your business offer a better deal than your competitors?
o   How much will it cost you to provide your product or service to the customer?
o   Who are your customers?
o   How will you increase the volume of your business?
o   What kinds of people will you need to hire? Can the work be done without these people?
o   Who are your competitors?
o   What do your competitors charge for the product or service you're offering?
o   Can you realistically provide this product or service at a higher level of quality or for a lower cost? If so, congratulations—you may be on to something that will work.

"Where there is no vision, the people perish." Proverbs 29:18 (KJV)

"And the Lord answered me, and said, Write the vision, and make it plain upon tables, that he may run that readeth it. For the vision is yet for an appointed time, but at the end it shall speak, and not lie: though it tarry, wait for it; because it will surely come, it will not tarry." Habakkuk 2:3 (KJV)

The Storehouse Principle

A lot of people disregard the storehouse principle, but it is a Bible-based principle. You may need to get a job and save at least 10 percent of your monthly income. With time it grows, and you can invest it wisely on in-formed investments to raise more money, which you can use to start your business. One of the best investments you can make is to buy secured land in a developing area and give it time to mature. This depends on how much you have saved. Whatever amount you have saved, you can always make your savings work for you, provided you make sound and informed investments.

"The LORD shall command the blessing upon thee in thy store-houses, and in all that thou settest thine hand unto; and He shall bless thee in the land which the LORD thy God giveth thee." Deuteronomy 28:8 (KJV)

Your Number One Focus Should Be Customer Satisfaction

One surefire way to set your new business apart from established com-petitors is simply by being more friendly and personable than anyone else. Make it your primary objective to please your customers through quality results and friendly service. Try to understand what the cus-tomer wants. Find the best way to satisfy those wants. The main focus of any business is customer satisfaction. The secondary focus should then be quality, cost/profit, appearance, function of product/service, and so on. Whatever you do, do not make your customer angry. You need to make every customer feel respected. **Matthew 22:39 says: "And the second is like unto it, Thou shalt love thy neighbor as thyself." (KJV)**

John 13:34: "A new commandment I give unto you, That ye love one another, as I have loved you, that ye also love one another." (KJV)

Offer Better Value than Competitors

Consumers want value for their money and abhor the idea of being "ripped off." Take advantage of this! Offer a better deal than your competitors—doing the same work for cheaper is sure to give you a leg up. However, ensure your profit margins are protected when deciding on your business's pricing structure—you always need to pay your rent. Make good on your promises and never be tempted to engage in false advertising as it will ruin your business's reputation in no time.

Deuteronomy 25:15 says: "But thou shalt have a perfect and just weight, a perfect and just measure shalt thou have: that thy days may be lengthened in the land which the Lord thy God giveth thee." (KJV)

Romans 12:9: "Let love be without dissimulation. Abhor that which is evil: cleave to that which is good." (KJV)

Romans 13:10: "Love worketh no ill to his neighbor: therefore love is the fulfilling of the law." (KJV)

Validate Your Idea—Research and Test Your Ideas

Preparation and planning is vital before setting out on any business venture. If you can, look for opportunities to perform "test runs." In other words, presell the idea and see if it works. For instance, if you're thinking of opening a restaurant, first try cooking for a church or a social gathering event to see if you can handle the hectic atmosphere of a busy kitchen and to judge whether your food is well received. You may also want to try conducting a survey among potential customers to judge whether they would pay for your business idea.

Business plans are evolving documents. If the results of your research or testing contradict your current plans, don't be afraid to change your business plan or even start from scratch. Doing so can be frustrating, but it's far smarter than risking the failure of your business on an idea that won't fly.

"Can two people walk together without agreeing on the direction? Does a lion roar in a thicket without first finding a victim? Does a young lion growl in its den without first catching its prey? Does a bird ever get caught in a trap that has no bait? Does a tarp ever spring shut when there's nothing there to catch?" Amos 3:3–5 (NLT)

Find Opportunities to Build Skills Cheaply

If you have an idea for a business but you lack the skills or training to pursue it, get the training you need for as cheap as possible. Try to make deals with those who can help you, and acquire knowledge from them. Take on a paid internship or apprenticeship part-time. Look for opportunities to gain practical know-how from friends, family, and skilled acquaintances. You should maintain a source of income while you're doing this—if this means you need to stretch your training over a longer length of time, please do so. If you need to go back to school, do so.

Proverbs 19:20: "Hear counsel, and receive instruction, that thou mayest be wise in thy latter end." (KJV)

Proverbs 20:18: "Every purpose is established by counsel: and with good advice make war." (KJV)

Proverbs 24:6: "For by wise counsel thou shalt make thy war: and in the multitude of counselors there is safety." (KJV)

Make the Most of Your Existing Assets and Let Your Creativity Replace Your Money

When you're starting a new business from nothing, you should use the resources you already have at your disposal as much as you can. If you have a home, use it as the initial site of your business, rather than renting an office. This way, you'll save the money you would otherwise have spent on rent. You can turn your garage into a workshop or start from your room. Some of today's biggest companies (most famously, Apple and Facebook) began in humble places: garages, basements, and dorm rooms, for instance. Ensure you make the most of what you have.

At the beginning, try to make sure your business is as lean as it can be. Minimize your need for cash, which can be hard to come by at first, and aggressively increase sales activity through developing and implementing your own creative ideas and concepts. Always think big. One great idea can be worth its weight in gold. **Isaiah 60:22: "A little one shall become a thousand, and a small one a strong nation: I the LORD will hasten it in his time." (KJV)**

Zechariah 4:10a: "Do not despise these small beginnings, for the LORD rejoices to see the work begin. To see the plumb line in Zerubbabel's hand." (NLT)

Ask Internet Users, Friends, and/or Family for a Loan

So you don't have an angel investor or a trust fund. This doesn't necessarily mean it'll be impossible to raise cash for your dream start-up! Today, it's easier than ever for people who have great ideas (but no money) to get the attention of people with money (but no great ideas). You may consider taking advantage of unconventional sources of funding—for instance, advertising your project on a crowdfunding site like Kickstarter. Sites like this allow you to "pitch" your idea to the Internet at large; if people online think your idea's good and your business plan is sound, they'll have the option of chipping in some of your start-up costs.

When attempting to build a business from scratch, your creativity and hard work can take the place of a substantial amount of money. However, you may reach a point where you simply can't proceed without a *little* money. For instance, you may need a certain expensive piece of equipment that you don't own and can't borrow. Many small businesses find their feet with help from a kind relative, a friend or even a neutral person who is interested in your business idea. Before you agree to a loan, however, make sure you specify the terms of the loan in writing: how long you will have to pay the loan back, how much your payments will be, etc. Depending on the country where you live, you may also secure an official small business loan from the government, if you meet the requirements. Many governments offer loan programs specifically designed to get small businesses off the ground. Financial institutions can also lend you small business loans.

Another way to win cash for your small business is to enter yourself in a start-up competition. These competitions are available in some countries and allow young, enterprising entrepreneurs to sell their ideas to wealthy venture capitalists. In these competitions, the winners usually win an initial round of funding to start their business!

Mark 9:23: "Jesus said unto him, if thou canst believe, all things are possible to him that believeth." (KJV)

Get the Word Out

The best-run business in the world will fail if nobody knows it exists. Here's your chance to make up for a lack of capital with your own hard work. If you can't afford to run TV ads or rent billboard space, try printing off flyers at home and handing them out on weekends. Go door-to-door advertising your business in the neighborhood. Make your own banner to hang from the front of your business. Dress up in a ridiculous costume and stand with a sign on a busy street corner. If you're not too proud, there are a lot of eye-catching things you can do to get the word out about your new business. If money's tight, your ego might have to take a backseat to your initial marketing efforts.

Today, you also have the potential to reach your customers online via a successful social media campaign. Social media is an effective way for a small business to represent itself to its customers online. Best of all, it's free for your business to join almost all major social media sites. Open an account on Facebook, Twitter, or other social networks, and encourage your customers to add you to their online circle (possibly by offering small perks to customers who do so) so that you can notify them about deals and promotions. Keep in mind, however, that online customers are used to being constantly bombarded with ads. Try to make your online content genuinely funny or striking—you'll be more popular than if you use social media solely as a platform for ads. **Luke 11:33: "No man, when he hath lighted a candle, putteth it in a secret place, neither under a bushel, but on a candlestick, that they which come in may see the light." (KJV)**

Be Diligent. Exhibit Passion and Determination

Starting your own business can be very hard—especially in the beginning—but if there is a genuine gap in the market and it's something you have a passion for, the work becomes much easier. If your passion for your work is so great and the money comes naturally while you're enjoying what you're doing, you can be confident that you've picked something that's perfect for you. When you have passion for your work, it's easy to keep your sense of determination strong because you won't be satisfied with yourself until you've done your best! Find some areas you are passionate about and grow your skills in those areas through studies, training courses, and the practical application of knowledge and skill. Find ways to make money out of your passion rather than trying to "force" the day job that you work to pay your bills into being the object of your passion.

When you start your own business, you may find that you need to make drastic changes to your habits and even your basic demeanor, to keep up with your new demands. Flexibility is a great asset if you're a new small business owner, as you may have to "reinvent" yourself a few times to find the niche you have chosen. Remember, starting your own business requires long hours and *lots* of focus. Change your behavior to ensure you're able to give your new job the time and attention that it needs. For instance, are you "not a morning person"? Are you "low energy"? If your restaurant's grand opening is in one week, you can't afford to be these things anymore! Change your habits *today*—set your alarm clock extra early and drink a big mug of coffee. **Proverbs 12:27: "The slothful man roasteth not that which he took in hunting: but the substance of a diligent man is precious." (KJV)**

Proverbs 22:29: "Seest thou a man diligent in his business? He shall stand before kings; he shall not stand before mean men." (KJV)

Dictionary.com defines *diligent* as "constant in effort to accomplish something; attentive and persistent in doing anything."

Approach Contracts and Partnerships with Caution

Be sure that you consider every business relationship or partnership you make very carefully. Only hire or partner with people you trust absolutely. If you do decide to partner with a person or business you trust, be sure to have the terms of your partnership recorded in writing *before* making your relationship official. It can be a *very* good idea to pay a lawyer to help you write your contracts. Legal fees can be expensive, but a well-written contract can save you many times your initial investment in the long run by preventing your partners from taking advantage of you.

Matthew 20:13: "But he answered one of them, and said, Friend, I do thee no wrong: didst not thou agree with me for a penny?" (KJV)

Build Your Ability to Negotiate

When all else fails, negotiate, barter, and trade. Confident, crafty bargaining ability is one of the defining traits of a true entrepreneur. This is a valuable skill to build, as it strengthens your innate business know-how and improves your confidence. Whether you're hiring a new employee, shopping for some equipment, or hammering out a business partnership, don't be afraid to haggle and make offers that are beneficial to you—the worst the other person can do is say "no." Take risks (while protecting your legal rights) and you may be pleasantly surprised at the outcome. **Matthew 19:26: "But Jesus beheld them, and said unto them, With men this is impossible; but with God all things are possible." (KJV)**

Rely on Your Family, Friends, and Loved Ones

You don't have to go this road alone, even if you don't make business partnerships with your loved ones (which can be a smart idea), you can lean on these people in the beginning (and later, when times are hard). Family and friends can offer powerful emotional support during your entrepreneurial journey. When you're stressed to your limit, this support can make the difference between pushing yourself to succeed and throwing in the towel. Talk to your family and make sure they agree with your overall business plan, because you may have to tax your family's resources, time, money, health, and nerves. It's only fair that they know what they're getting into.

Ecclesiastes 4:9: "Two are better than one; because they have a good reward for their labor." (KJV)

Amos 3:3: "Can two walk together, except they be agreed?" (KJV)

Know Your Rights

Having sound knowledge of commercial law (especially contract law, tax law, and the legal requirements for running a small business) is a valuable skill for an entrepreneur to have. If possible, it's a great idea to familiarize yourself with these areas of law before starting your business. If you're truly confident in these areas of law, you can save money. However, if you're *not* familiar with the law, get help. The money you spend on a lawyer can save you many times your initial investment—for instance, by preventing you from getting into damaging contracts. You'll also spare yourself from serious headaches when trying to decipher complex business and tax documents.

Proverbs 11:14: "**Where no counsel is, the people fall: but in the multitude of counselors there is safety.**" (KJV)

Proverbs 12:15: "**The way of a fool is right in his own eyes: but he that harkeneth unto counsel is wise.**" (KJV)

Proverbs 15:22: "**Without counsel purposes are disappointed: but in the multitude of counselors they are established.**" (KJV)

Look After Your Physical, Mental, and Emotional State

If you lose your health, you may lose it all. A healthy body, mind, and soul are vital to success as a business owner. Especially in the beginning, the hours may be *very* long and the work may be *very* hard. Still, you should always try to devote reasonable amounts of time to exercise, sleep, and downtime. Treat these things with the respect they deserve—they keep you healthy and sane. Remember, if you're incapacitated, you can't run your business. Do all things in moderation and live life with a sense of balance, even when you're starting a business with barely any money in the bank. Losing your perspective in life will make you poorer in the long run (emotionally—not necessarily financially), so it's never a risk worth taking. Never miss a night's sleep. Don't work yourself to death. Always devote time to your family, your hobbies, and, of course, yourself. Your life should be a source of joy and passion, not just an opportunity to work.

Additionally, you should never rely on drugs to aid your performance, ability, or to replace your regular healthy eating and exercise plans. This will, in the long run, break you down and cause you to make irrational, emotional decisions, which are never a good thing in business.

Ecclesiastes 2:24: "**There is nothing better for a man, than that he should eat and drink, and that he should make his soul to enjoy good in his labor. This also I saw, that it was from the hand of God.**" (KJV)

Ecclesiastes 3:13: "And also that every man should eat and drink, and enjoy the good of all his labor, it is the gift of God." (KJV)

Ecclesiastes 5:18: "Behold that which I have seen: it is good and comely for one to eat and to drink, and to enjoy the good of all his labor that he taketh under the sun all the days of his life, which God giveth him: for it is his portion." (KJV)

1Timothy 4:8: "For bodily exercise profiteth little: but godliness is profitable unto all things, having promise of the life now is, and of that which is to come." (KJV)

The Bible advises that bodily exercise profits little, but my advice for you is: take that little exercise. It is good for your body and soul.

Chapter Fourteen

How to Enjoy Financial Freedom

Financial freedom happens only when we put our trust in the living God and not in uncertain riches. Financial security without trust in God brings fear and sorrow with it. **"The blessing of the LORD, it maketh rich, and he addeth no sorrow with it." Proverbs 10:22 (KJV)**

> **"Both riches and honor come of thee, and thou reignest over all; and in thine hand is power and might; and in thine hand it is to make great, and to give strength unto all." 1 Chronicles 29:12 (KJV)**

The Lord said that those who trust in Him would not lack any good thing **(Psalm 34:10).** This includes a successful business and financial freedom. **Psalm 23:1 says, "The Lord is my shepherd, I shall not want."**

Trusting in your money or in the world's financial system is a recipe for disaster. **It's not in man to direct his own steps (Jeremiah 10:23).** There's a better way, and that's God's way.

"But thou shalt remember the Lord thy God: for it is He that giveth thee power to get wealth, that he may establish his covenant which he sware unto thy fathers, as it is this day." Deuteronomy 8:18 (KJV)

God is the One who gives us power to get wealth. Notice that He doesn't give us wealth directly. He gives us the power or ability (ideas, talent, skill, knowledge, health, etc.) to acquire wealth. Whether you realize it or not, God is the source of your ideas, abilities and prosperity.

Let me ask you this question: Are you the one who provided the life you have—the ability, talent, and skill? We didn't give ourselves talents and abilities. We can develop our talents, but each one of us has gifts that were given to us by God. We can't develop what God didn't give us.

If you were asked to pay for every breath of fresh air you took, you could not afford it. If you had some debilitating handicap, you would not be able to work. So, again I say, whether you realize it or not, God is the source of prosperity.

Financial prosperity and freedom isn't God giving you money. He gives you an anointing (favor) that enables you to prosper. The real asset is not the money—nor the house, the car, or the physical tangible things. It is the anointing (favor) from God that produces the wealth. The real asset is the favor of God. Money isn't prosperity; money is the by-product of prosperity. Many people fall into the trap of measuring financial freedom by the amount of money or things they have. Being prosperous is relying on God as your source.

There are people who prosper without trusting God, but it usually destroys their lives. They have hardship, stress, marital problems, sickness, and on and on without solution. **"But they that will be rich fall into temptation and a snare, and into many foolish and hurtful lusts, which drown men in destruction and perdition. For the love of money is the root of all evil: which while some coveted after, they have erred from the faith, and pierced themselves through with many sorrows." 1 Timothy 6:9–10 (KJV)**

They might be rich, but it has cost them in other areas. Many of them end up losing it all, including their lives. Notice that the Bible did not say that money is the root of all evil; rather it says the love of money is the root of all evil. We are not asked to love money but to love God and people. It is important to note that not trusting God is the actual root of all evil.

Jesus said in John 10:10: **"The thief cometh not, but for to steal, and to kill, and to destroy: I am come that they might have life, and that they might have it more abundantly."** This is true freedom.

To enjoy financial freedom we must be rich toward God and help the needy. We must understand that when we give to God and people in need, we are not giving anything away; rather, we position ourselves to receive something infinitely greater than what we gave. A good example is the woman at the well. Jesus asked this woman for water not because He wanted to take anything away from her but because He wanted to bless her beyond measure. **"Jesus answered and said unto her, if thou knowest the gift of God, and who it is that saith to thee, Give me to drink; thou wouldest have asked of him, and he would have given thee living water." John 4:10 (KJV)**

Can you see in the above scripture that God expects you to ask because the authority has been given to you and you must exercise that authority by asking? He loves you unconditionally and will not deny anything good from you. All you need to do is to trust Him, ask and receive that your joy may be full. **"Hitherto have ye asked nothing in my name: ask, and ye shall receive, that your joy may be full." John 16:24 (KJV)**

The story of the rich, young ruler is a good example of someone God wanted to bless beyond measure, if only he could trust Him. **"Then Jesus beholding him loved him, and said unto him, One thing thou lackest: go thy way, sell whatsoever thou hast, and give to the poor, and thou shalt have treasure in heaven: and come, take up the cross, and follow me." Mark 10:21 (KJV)**

Jesus loved this man and wanted to help him. In the man's heart, he was trusting in money, and Jesus was trying to help him shift his trust to God.

When the young man heard Jesus ask him to sell everything he had and give the proceeds to the poor, he hung his head and walked away. He knew in his heart that he couldn't do it. After the man left, the disciples began asking Jesus questions about what He had just taught regarding money.

"And the disciples were astonished at his words. But Jesus answereth again, and saith unto them, Children, how hard is it for them that trust in riches to enter into the kingdom of God! It is easier for a

camel to go through the eye of a needle, than for a rich man to enter into the kingdom of God." Mark 10:24–25 (KJV)

The Issue is Trust in God not Money or Our Abilities

As we can see in verse twenty-four, the issue at hand is trust in God and not the man's money or his abilities in keeping the law because no man can successfully keep the law. Man cannot save himself, he needs a Savior. Jesus said how hard it is for those **who trust in riches** to enter into the kingdom of God. Note that the kingdom of God simply means God's ways of doing things—faith, godliness, righteousness, love, patience, meekness, peace, and joy in the Holy Spirit. Again notice that Jesus said it is easier for a camel to go through the eye of a needle than for those who trust in their riches to enter into the kingdom of God. In other words, it is impossible. The problem here is that their faith has been shifted to their money and not God. Trusting in our riches always leads to impossibility. **Hebrews 11:6 says: "But without faith it is impossible to please him: for he that cometh to God must believe that he is, and that he is a rewarder of them that diligently seek him."**

"And he spake a parable unto them, saying, The ground of a certain rich man brought forth plentifully: And he thought within himself, saying what shall I do, because I have no room where to bestow my fruits? And he said, This will I do: I will pull down my barns, and build greater; and there will I bestow all my fruits and my goods. And I will say to my soul, Soul thou hast much goods laid up for many years: take thine ease, eat, drink, and be merry. But God said unto him, Thou fool, this night thy soul shall be required of thee: then whose shall those things be, which thou hast provided? So is he that layeth up treasure for himself, and is not rich toward God." Luke 12:16–21 (KJV)

Here we see it again. This rich man was not rich toward God (He was not a giver to the poor and needy) and his end was sad, just like the rich young ruler. As you can see, trusting in our riches leads to lack of faith or trust in God and always leads to sorrow.

The scripture is not saying that rich men will not enter into the kingdom of God—Abraham was rich and he entered. It's talking about rich people who put their trust in their riches and will not use it to serve God or help others in need.

"There was a certain rich man, which was clothed in purple and fine linen, and fared sumptuously every day: And there was a certain beggar named Lazarus, which was laid at his gate, full of sores, And desiring to be fed with the crumbs which fell from the rich man's table: moreover the dogs came and licked his sores. And it came to pass, that the beggar died, and was carried by the angels into Abraham's bosom: the rich man also died, and was buried; And in hell he lift up his eyes, being in torments, and seeth Abraham afar off, and Lazarus in his bosom. And he cried and said, Father Abraham, have mercy on me, and send Lazarus, that he may dip the tip of his finger in water, and cool my tongue; for I am tormented in this flame. But Abraham said, Son, remember that thou in thy lifetime receivedst thy good things, and likewise Lazarus evil things: but now he is comforted, and thou art tormented. And beside all this, between us and you there is a great gulf fixed: so that they which would pass from hence to you cannot; neither can they pass to us, that would come from thence. Then he said, I pray thee therefore, father, that thou wouldest send him to my father's house: For I have five brethren; that he may testify unto them, lest they also come into this place of torment. Abraham saith unto him, They have Moses and the prophets; let them hear them. And he said, Nay, father Abraham: but if one went unto them from the dead, they will repent. And he said unto him, If they hear not Moses and the prophets, neither will they be persuaded, though one rose from the dead." Luke 16:19–31(KJV)

"Money is a defense but it cannot give life. Only God can give life. For wisdom is a defense, and money is a defense: but the excellency of knowledge is, that wisdom giveth life to them that have it." Ecclesiastes 7:12 (KJV) Wisdom is to trust in God and not riches, which cannot save. Finally, Jesus said to them:

"Verily I say unto you, There is no man that hath left house, or brethren, or sisters, or father, or mother, or wife, or children, or lands, for my sake, and the gospel's, But he shall receive a hundredfold now in this time, houses, and brethren, and sisters, and mothers, and children, and lands, with persecutions; and in the world to come eternal life." Mark 10:29 (KJV)

Jesus said this right after they saw the rich, young ruler walk away. In other words, if the man had sold everything he had and given it to the poor, he would have received a hundredfold return in this life. As always, Jesus wasn't trying to take anything away from the man. He needed the man's faith to bless him back beyond measure—a hundred times over. You're a steward, and the money you have isn't really yours anyway (it's God that gave you ideas, life, talent, ability, health, etc.), but God is never going to let you out-give Him. When you do give, the Lord will always bless you back—not just in heaven, but here on Earth, too.

The rich man's refusal to sell his possessions revealed the true condition of his heart. He thought Jesus was trying to take something away from Him. His trust in money was a hindrance to his relationship with God—money was his god and his trust in the money made it impossible for him to enter into the kingdom of God. He would rather disobey Jesus and keep his money.

There are many verses that talk about God blessing us and prospering us when we give; it's an established principle in the Word of God. If you aren't giving to God and others in need, then you either don't know His promises to give back to you, or you don't really trust Him or believe those promises are true. When you give to God you're not giving to the pastor or the church; it's a relationship between you and God and you must see it as such. Remember that the Devil will never ask you to give or tithe. He will not even ask you to go to church.

Just as Jesus used money to reveal the rich man's attitude, you can see what is in a person's heart by looking at how they operate financially toward God and others.

Jesus didn't ask every rich person He met to sell everything they owned. He went to the house of a very wealthy tax collector named Zacchaeus and never mentioned money—and tax collectors earned a lot of money by stealing from people. **(Luke 19:2–9)** Zacchaeus decided to give half of his goods to the poor and to restore four times any money he had stolen, but Jesus didn't ask him to do those things; Zacchaeus did them voluntarily. Jesus didn't ask everyone to sell all they had because the issue isn't money—it's whether or not you are trusting in your money instead of God. The issue is trust. Zacchaeus had faith (trust) in God and he received salvation, unlike the rich young ruler.

Jesus used finances to demonstrate to the rich young ruler the true condition of his heart. Remember, Jesus said that **"If we aren't faithful in that which is least, then we won't be faithful in something greater." Luke 16:10 (KJV)**

The question is why should we even give anything to God in the first instance because there is nothing we can give to God that He does not already have? He owns everything, including our lives. The answer is that He needs our faith to come through for us. Without faith it is impossible to please God. Giving is one major way we demonstrate our faith in Him. God is a spirit; it is only through our faith that we can receive everything He has provided for us in the realm of the spirit. So the issue is not money but faith in God or trust in God through our giving. When we give to God, we are the ones who are changed. Never forget that. We must always relate to God based on faith and nothing else. Also we are God's extended hand to the poor and needy. When we give to them we are giving to God.

If you help the poor, you are lending to the Lord—and he will repay you! (Prov. 19:17 NLT).

He that giveth unto the poor shall not lack: but he that hideth his eyes shall have many a curse. (Prov. 28:27 KJV)

Paul and Silas praised God in prison and God came through for them—the prison doors opened on their own. It was a praise of faith. The Bible says in **James 5:15**: **"And the prayer of faith shall save the sick, and the Lord shall raise him up; and if he have committed sins, they shall be forgiven him." (KJV)** Again it's the prayer of faith and not just prayer. So if you have faith in God, the giving of faith will also naturally follow.

God gives us the ability to make money because we need it to function in this world. We use it to buy the goods that meet our needs, but money is not what provides for us. It is the favor of God on us. The question is whether we are trusting in God as the source of our provision, or whether we are operating out of fear and trusting in money itself. Money is just a delivery system; God is our source and provider. We are custodians of God's wealth and must use it to serve God and help the needy. This knowledge is what gives financial freedom.

Jesus told the rich man to sell everything he had in an effort to reveal the condition of his heart.

If Jesus was still on Earth in His physical body today, He would be asking whether our trust is in God or in welfare, human connections, stocks, bonds, and pension funds. He would be urging us to administer our finances as stewards—because He is the one who gave it to us, and to put our trust in Him.

God wants all of you and not your money. He wants to bless you more and give you something infinitely better than money: peace of mind, which money cannot buy. The way God gets you to trust Him in that area of your life is by asking you to give a portion of what you earn back to Him and to others, and He promises to bless you in return beyond measure. But you need to believe this for it to work for you, because without faith it is impossible to please God. Giving to God helps you remember that the power to achieve wealth comes from God, and it teaches you to trust God as your true source of prosperity. You have to trust that God has your best interests at heart.

"If therefore ye have not been faithful in the unrighteous mammon, who will commit to your trust the true riches? And if ye have not been faithful in that which is another man's, who shall give you that which is your own? No servant can serve two masters: for either he will hate the one, and love the other; or else he will hold to the one, and despise the other. Ye cannot serve God and mammon." Luke 16:11–13 (KJV)

Mammon means money. Jesus is saying that trusting God with your finances is the least important area in which to trust God. When Jesus said in **Luke 16:10, "He that is faithful in that which is least," He was calling money "that which is least."** God provided healing, deliverance, salvation, and prosperity through His Son, Jesus, over two thousand years ago. These gifts become a reality for us when we mix them with faith because faith appropriates what God has already provided. You can't buy healing or any other blessing of God. You can only receive from God by faith. Faith is the only thing that makes anything God has done for us manifest in our lives.

It's not a matter of pleasing God with giving before He will heal you or bless you. It's all about being able to trust Him for small things before you try trusting Him for big things. If you can't trust God with your money, how can you say you trust Him in other areas of your life? The point here is trust.

People talk about money being true riches, but this is not true because the real problems in life are problems that money cannot solve, like a child that is afflicted, a marriage that is not working, or a medical condition that has no cure. Money is nothing compared to health. People pay so much money trying to get well. Anyone who has ever been really sick can tell you that good health is priceless. If one has a money problem all the person needs is either to wait and work for the money, or ask people for help. A lot of people will be willing to assist depending on how they are approached. But if one has a terminal disease, it's only a matter of time before the person dies. This is why money problems are not the worst human problems. Money is limited in power—it cannot give life or permanent security. In the same way, believing for your family to be restored, for healing to manifest in your body, or for mental and emotional healing are all infinitely greater than believing for finances. If you haven't trusted God with your finances yet, how can you go beyond that and trust Him to heal your body? How will you trust God to get over depression if you can't do that which is least and trust Him with your money? How can you trust God to give you eternal life, but not trust Him with your money so he can bless you in return and provide for your physical needs? Remember, the Word says that you can't serve two masters. **(Luke 16:13)**

You can't trust yourself when it comes to money and then try to trust God with everything else. It isn't effective to compartmentalize your faith so that you are trusting God in one area, but not in others. If you are going to trust God, then trust Him all the way. The same God who promised eternal life when you confess Jesus as your Lord, and believe in your heart that God raised Him from the dead **(Romans 10:9)**, also said to give and it would be given back to you **(Luke 6:38)**. The same God who promised that He would save you and give you eternal life also promised to prosper you financially. It's double-minded **(James 1:7–8)** to say that you will trust God with your eternal salvation and healing for your body, but not trust Him enough to give your money to Him and see yourself as a steward of God's resources.

Finances are the lowest use of your faith. It helps you trust God as your source. God has a plan for your life. Start from a position of stewardship, and let Him be the owner. You will be abundantly blessed and enjoy financial freedom.

Now you want to start a successful business but you have no money. This is a very good place to start from if you do not know what to do. Trust God with what you have and ask Him what you can give and where to give it as a demonstration of your faith in His ability to provide for you, and see what God will do in your business life. It's not about the amount you give but rather to show that your trust is in Him. Remember that He has already provided for you. So you're not giving to get rich because you're already rich rather you're giving to activate your faith and receive the riches God has already deposited inside you in the spiritual realm and to show your trust in God in that regard.

"He raiseth up the poor out of the dust, and lifteth the needy out of the dunghill." Psalm 113:7 (KJV)

At this point you may ask what percentage of my income should I give to God? He answers us in **Leviticus 27:32: "And concerning the tithe of the herd, or of the flock, even of whatsoever passeth under the rod, the tenth shall be holy unto the LORD."**

Tithe is also mentioned in the newtestament - **Matthew 23:23: "Woe unto you, scribes and Pharisees, hypocrites! For ye pay tithe of mint and anise and cumin, and have omitted the weightier matters of the law, judgment, mercy, and faith: these ought ye to have done, and not to leave the other undone."** You can see from the above scripture that to tithe without faith (trusting God) is hypocrisy. It does not work. Tithe is also mentioned in **Hebrews 7:1–2: "For this Melchisedec, king of Salem, priest of the most high God, who met Abraham returning from the slaughter of the kings, and blessed him; To whom also Abraham gave a tenth part of all; first being by interpretation king of righteousness, and after that also king of Salem, which is, king of peace."**

This is a good place to start. As you give, God allows you to give more. There are testimonies of people who gave away up to 60 percent of their income and still had much abundance. For instance, Zacchaeus gave away half of his worth to the poor and also promised to restore four-fold to anyone he had cheated in a single meeting with Jesus. I believe that Zacchaeus experienced much more wealth and greater ability to give after this act of faith because you can never out-give God when you give in faith.

You Can Never Out-Give God

The following testimony proves that you can never out-give God. It is an excerpt taken from the book -You Can't Beat God Giving: Miracle Testimonies from Ordinary People Serving an extraordinary God - by Evangelist R. W. Schambach:

"I'll never forget, the greatest miracle I ever witnessed began with an offering. It happened under the ministry of Brother A. A. Allen.

I was with this man of God for about five years in the fifties. . ."

".... A woman brought her child, who had twenty-six major diseases, to our meeting. I'll never forget this as long as I live.

The boy was born blind, deaf and mute. Both arms were crippled and deformed. His elbows protruded up into his little tummy; his knees touched his elbows. Both legs were crippled and deformed; he had club feet. When he was born, his doctors said that boy would never live to see his first birthday, but they were wrong; he was approaching four years of age. Of course, his condition was breaking his mama's heart. She came to our meetings all week, and I got concerned about that boy. In those crusades, we had each person with a need fill out a prayer card, and as the Holy Spirit moved, we would pray for the needs God inspired us to pray for. And the Holy Spirit didn't seem to be moving us to pray for that little boy."

"The following Sunday, his mother came to me and said, 'Brother Schambach, I'm down to my last twenty dollars. I've paid the hotel bill, but we've been eating in the restaurant, coming to three services a day and giving in every offering. All the money has run out. My baby has not been prayed for.' She was very upset, and she was ready to give up and go home."

"I said 'Ma'am, I can't apologize for the moving of the Holy Ghost. I know you have to leave tonight, but if you come to the service and, once again, the Holy Spirit leads in another direction, and your son's prayer card is not drawn for prayer, I will personally take your baby to the man of God's trailer house and see that he lays hands on your baby. You will not leave disappointed.' And I meant that from my heart." "That night I came out, and I led the singing in that evening service. Then I introduced Brother A. A. Allen, and he came bouncing out on that platform and said 'Tonight we're going to receive an offering of faith.' I had never heard him use that expression before, and I saw eyebrows lift all over the congregation. He went on, 'Now, if you don't know what I mean when I say an 'offering of faith,' I mean for you to give God something you cannot afford to give. That's a good definition, isn't it? If you can afford it, there's no faith connected to it. So give Him something you can't afford to give.'"

"As soon as Brother Allen said that, I saw that boy's mother leap out into the aisle and come running. Three thousand people were watching her in that Birmingham Fairgrounds Arena as she threw something in that offering bucket. I never saw anybody in such a hurry to give, and, I confess, I was nosy. I came down off that platform to see what she had given. You know what I saw in that bucket? A twenty dollar bill."

"I knew that was all she had. She had told me that. She had driven from Knoxville, Tennessee, to the meeting in Birmingham, Alabama. She didn't know how she was going to get home or what she was going to use to feed herself and her baby on the way. I went behind the platform and wept. I prayed, 'Lord, I've been trying to teach that woman faith all week. But now I'm asking You to give me faith like she's got!'"

". . . Brother Allen went on and collected the offering and launched into his sermon. But about fifteen minutes into his message he stopped and said, 'I'm being carried away in the Spirit.'" "I said to myself, 'Here we go again on another trip.' This is how God used him: he said he could see what the Holy Spirit wanted to communicate to him like he was watching it on a television screen. He would describe it as he saw it. That night he said, 'I'm being carried away to a huge white building. Oh, it's a hospital.' Of course, I heard this kind of thing every night that I worked with Brother Allen so I was sitting there unmoved." "Then he said, 'I'm inside the hospital, and there's no doubt in my mind where I'm heading because I hear all these babies crying. It's a maternity ward. I see five doctors around a table. A little baby has been born. The baby was born with twelve, no, sixteen, no, twenty-six diseases.'"

"When he said that, I started getting chill bumps up and down my spine. I said, 'Oh, my God, tonight's that baby's night!'" "Brother Allen continued, 'Twenty-six diseases. The doctors said he'd never live to see his first birthday, but that's not so. That boy is approaching four. Now I see the mother packing a suitcase.

They're going on a trip. Another lady's with her. The baby's in a bassinet. It's in the back seat of an old Ford. They're driving down the highway. I see the Alabama/Tennessee border. That automobile is driving in the parking lot. Lady you're here tonight. Bring me that baby! God's going to give you twenty-six miracles.'"

"That woman came running again for the second time that night. She put the baby in Brother Allen's arms. I jumped up to stand beside him, and everybody in the audience, 3,000 strong, was standing. Brother Allen must have wanted to be sure that the audience was agreeing in faith for the miracle because he said, 'Everybody, close your eyes.' But I thought, 'Not me, mister. I'm going to be scriptural on this one. I'm going to watch and pray. I've been waiting for this all week. '"

"That little boy's tongue had been hanging out of his mouth all week. The first thing I saw as Brother Allen prayed was that tongue snapped back in the mouth like a rubber band. For the first time in four years, the little guy's tongue was in his mouth. I saw two little whirlpools in his eyes, just a milky color. You couldn't tell whether he had blue or brown or what color of eyes.

But during the prayer, that whirlpool ceased, and I saw two brand new brown eyes! I knew God had opened his eyes, and if God opened the eyes, I knew He had unstopped the deaf ears." "Then those little arms began to snap like pieces of wood; and for the first time, they stretched out. The legs cracked like wood popping. All of sudden, I saw God form toes out of those club feet as easily as child forms something with silly-putty. The crowd was watching by this time going wild! I've never seen any people shout and rejoice so much in all my life."

"I saw that baby placed on his feet, and he began to run for the first time in his life. He had never seen his mama before, never said a word, but he began running across the platform and I was running right after him to catch him. He leaped into his mama's arms, and I heard him say his first word, 'Mama.'"

" . . . . The following Saturday after his healing, I received a special delivery letter from his mother. . . She said 'Brother Schambach, I took the baby to the hospital Monday morning, and the doctors won't give him back. They kept him all week. They have called in every doctor from all over the country who has had anything to do with the case. They have pronounced my baby cured of twenty-six major diseases.' Of course, we went on to get the copies of the affidavits from the doctors certifying that boy's life was a genuine miracle."

"Her letter continued, 'You remember that last Sunday when I told you all I had was twenty dollars? God knows that was the truth.

But when that man of God said to give something you can't afford, I leaped into the aisle. The moment I hit that aisle, for the first time in my life I heard the devil talk. The devil told me, 'You can't give that; that's not yours. Fifteen dollars of that goes to the doctor. Five dollars is for gas to get home.' The faster I ran, the faster he talked. But as soon as I turned loose of that money, he stopped talking.'

"'Brother Schambach, all you saw was those twenty-six miracles, but there is one you don't know anything about. After you were gone, people were staying there. They wanted to see the baby and see what God had done. People shook hands with me. When one lady shook my hands, I felt a folded piece of paper between my palms. I opened it up and saw it was a twenty dollar bill. As I shook hands with the people who had lined up, every one of them had a folded paper in their hand. I went into the ladies room and counted $235!'"

The $20 produced 26 miracles and $235. Indeed, you can never out-give God.

"But this I say, He which soweth sparingly shall reap also sparingly; and he which soweth bountifully shall reap also bountifully. Every man according as he purposeth in his heart, so let him give; not grudgingly, or of necessity: for God loveth a cheerful giver. And God is able to make all grace abound toward you; that ye, always having all sufficiency in all things, may abound to every good work." 2 Corinthians 9:6–9 (KJV)

In your giving it is important not to give out of emotion. God is only accessible by faith and not emotions. Sometimes people say they gave to

God but did not receive anything in return. The reason is because they did not give in faith. Most times, they give in fear or out of emotion and compulsion. The Bible says God is a rewarder of them who diligently seek him.

"But without faith it is impossible to please Him: for he that cometh to God must believe that he is, and that He is a rewarder of them that diligently seek Him." Hebrews 11:6 (KJV)

When you're not sure what to give, ask Him and He will direct you. **"In all thy ways acknowledge Him, and He shall direct thy paths." Psalm 3:6 (KJV)** This includes in your giving. When you give in faith you will always have peace of mind and great return from your giving.

When God is your source, He will supply all of your needs with peace of mind. And it won't be according to this world's economy, with all its depressions and recessions. **Matthew 6:18–19** puts it this way: **"Lay not up for yourselves treasures upon earth, where moth and rust doth corrupt, and where thieves break through and steal: But lay up for yourselves treasures in heaven, where moth nor rust doth corrupt, and where thieves do not break through nor steal."** Is God telling us here not to work hard and save money for our needs? Not at all, because **2 Thessalonians 3:10** already told us: **"For even when we were with you, this we commanded you, that if any would not work, neither should he eat."** (KJV). It was God who told Joseph in **Genesis 41** to tell Pharaoh to save **20 percent** of all the produce in the seven years of plenty, which saved their lives during the seven years of famine. So God is not against us having riches. What God is telling us is not to put our trust in uncertain riches. The issue is where we put our trust. Trust God with what you have and your needs will be supplied according to God's economy, which is certain and reliable unlike the economy of the world. God can direct our path and let us know, at all times, how to avoid dangers that will destroy our wealth. This is financial freedom and it is wonderful.

"But my God shall supply all your need according to His riches in glory by Christ Jesus." Philippians 4:19 (KJV)

God says He'll supply all your need! And it's not going to be according to this world's system, where there is so much corruption and stealing. When God is your source, you will have not only supernatural ideas and prosperity but also a peace that many people of the world don't have.

When people tithe or give offering, many of them feel that they're giving from what they've earned. After all, they're the ones who put in the work to get a paycheck. But everything would change for them if they saw themselves as handling God's resources. Stewards are those who see themselves as accountable for what God has entrusted to them.

The Reason for Financial Prosperity

Trusting God with your finances is the baby step of faith to enjoying financial freedom. And if you can't trust Him with that which is least, then according to what Jesus said in **Luke 16**, He can't trust you with heavenly riches:

"He that is faithful in that which is least is faithful also in much: and he that is unjust in the least is unjust also in much. If therefore ye have not been faithful in the unrighteous mammon, who will commit to your trust the true riches?" Luke 16:10–11 (KJV)

If you understand financial stewardship properly, it will enable you to be a blessing to others. This allows God to channel more resources to you so you can help more people because now you serve as His helping hand to many. God loves to work through someone. Decide to be that person.

"God is able to make all grace abound toward you; that ye, always having all sufficiency in all things, may abound to every good work." 2 Corinthians 9:8 (KJV)

The reason God makes grace abound toward you is so that you will abound (give) to every good work. The real motive behind finances shouldn't be to get; it should be to give. This is a critical point.

Many people who reject teaching on biblical prosperity do so because they see it as selfish or greedy. They say, "I've got enough. I may not be rich, but I have a roof over my head and my basic needs are covered. I don't want or need any more." But that is a selfish attitude. If you have all you need, trust God for more so you can help others. This is the will and purpose of God for you. The thinking that says "I've got enough—forget everyone else" is the truly selfish attitude. We need to prosper, not so that we can have more, but so that we can be a bigger blessing to others.

The Lord told Abraham that He would bless him and make him a blessing **(Genesis 12:2)**. You can't give away what you don't have. Abraham couldn't be a blessing to others until he had been blessed by God. Whatever you have today—talent, ability, ideas, money—it's God that has given it to you.

You and I cannot fulfill God's purposes for our lives without receiving from Him. God's kingdom cannot advance without God's people prospering. We need this revelation. We need to know how to prosper God's way and enjoy financial freedom. The truth is that God has already prospered you, but you need to see it and receive it by faith. Then things will begin to improve, beyond your imagination, and you will enjoy true financial freedom by trusting Him with what you have received.

Chapter Fifteen

How to Be Happy in Life

Everyone longs for happiness, but few possess it. The pursuit of it is universal and timeless. For most people, however, happiness is elusive.

And he said unto them, Take heed, and beware of covetousness: for a man's life consisteth not in the abundance of the things which he possesseth (Lk. 12:15 KJV).

> **Then he said unto them, Go your way, eat the fat, and drink the sweet, and send portions unto them for whom nothing is prepared: for this day is holy unto our Lord: neither be ye sorry; for the joy of the Lord is your strength (Neh. 8:10 KJV).**

Notice that no joy, no strength. So, is true happiness obtainable? And if so, how do we get it?

First, let me say there are many scriptures that command us to rejoice and be glad.

But may all who search for you be filled with joy and gladness in you. May those who love your salvation repeatedly shout, "The LORD is great!"(Ps. 40:16 NLT)

But let the righteous be glad; let them rejoice before God: yea, let them exceedingly rejoice. (Ps. 68:3 KJV)

I have told you all this so that you may have peace in me. Here on earth you will have many trials and sorrows. But take heart, because I have overcome the world."(Jn. 16:33 NLT)

The apostle Paul wrote the book of Philippians while he was in prison in Rome. He was facing possible execution. Yet his letter to the Philippians is the happiest letter of any he wrote. He mentioned rejoicing in this short letter more than in any other of his letters. How could this be? What was Paul's secret? The book of Philippians gives us the keys Paul used to obtain such success.

I have learned, in whatsoever state I am, therewith to be content (Phil. 4:11 KJV).

While covetousness can destroy, contentment is the key to happiness.

Notice that contentment is something the apostle Paul learned. It didn't come naturally or without effort. None of us came out of the womb reading and writing; we had to learn through years of effort. Likewise, contentment, which is a major component of happiness, has to be learned. It doesn't come on us like a seizure, and we don't catch it like a cold. It is an acquired trait. So you must learn to frequently say to yourself, "I choose to be happy in Jesus's name." There is so much power in your words.

How do we acquire happiness? First, we need to deal with what's on the inside. Most people take a different approach. They want to deal with the outside. They pray for their problems to be solved and that only good things and good people will come their way. Let me give you a clue: that will not happen!

As long as we are in this world, we will have problems **(John 16:33)**. And if we are living for God, we will have persecutions **(2 Tim. 3:12)**.

You can't always control what goes on outside, but you can totally control what goes on inside when faced with resistance. When you understand that, you will have discovered one of the greatest keys to happiness. In addition, you will be on your way to eliminating grief in your life.

The Root of all Grief

Selfishness is at the root of all our grief. I know that's a hard pill to swallow for many, but that's because we live in a society that has learned to blame circumstances and other people rather than taking personal responsibility.

For example, it is very clear that the way others treat us is not the root of contentions; it's our pride:

> **Only by pride cometh contention: but with the well advised is wisdom (Prov. 13:10 KJV).**

If we weren't so in love with ourselves, so prideful and self-centered, we wouldn't be so sensitive to all the things that rub us the wrong way. It really comes down to our love of self. One of the most liberating things in the world is to love someone else more than you love yourself. And when the one you love more is God, you will rejoice when He is glorified, even if that happens through your suffering.

That's what Paul did. In Philippians 1, the apostle Paul was trying to comfort the Philippians. These were special people to Paul, and he was special to them. In **Philippians 4:15–16**, Paul said the Philippians were the only church that ever gave to him after he left their area. They did this not just once but twice, and they would have partnered with him more if they had known where he was.

He wanted to assure them that everything was all right with him. How did he do that? He told them that all his suffering had furthered the kingdom of God.

> **But I would ye should understand, brethren, that the things which happened unto me have fallen out rather unto the furtherance of the gospel;**
> **So that my bonds in Christ are manifest in all the palace, and in all other places;**
> **And many of the brethren in the Lord, waxing confident by my bonds, are much more bold to speak the word without fear.**

> **Some indeed preach Christ even of envy and strife; and some also of good will:**
> **The one preach Christ of contention, not sincerely, supposing to add affliction to my bonds:**
> **But the other of love, knowing that I am set for the defense of the gospel.**
> **What then? Notwithstanding, every way, whether in pretense, or in truth, Christ is preached; and I therein do rejoice, yea, and will rejoice (Phil. 1:12–18 KJV).**

That says volumes! Paul loved God and the furtherance of His kingdom more than he loved himself. If the Kingdom of God was better off because of Paul's imprisonment, then it was all worth it. What a great attitude. We would do well to adopt it.

Number One Obstacle to Contentment

When God and others are more important to you than yourself, then you are well on your way to happiness, but if you are all wrapped up in yourself, you make a very small package. And therein lies the number-one obstacle to contentment and happiness.

Most people are addicted to self like addicts are to drugs. They are never satisfied. And this self-centered dissatisfaction is Satan's greatest open door for temptation. He used self-interest to tempt Adam and Eve, even though they lived in a perfect world without a single problem.

> **But of the fruit of the tree which is in the midst of the garden, God hath said, Ye shall not eat of it, neither shall ye touch it, lest ye die.**
> **And the serpent said unto the woman, Ye shall not surely die:**
> **For God doth know that in the day ye eat thereof, then your eyes shall be opened, and ye shall be as gods, knowing good and evil (Gen. 3:3–5 KJV).**

Even Jesus's disciples weren't satisfied with Him. Despite all they had seen Him do, they still wanted more outward proof of who He was.

Philip saith unto him, Lord, show us the Father, and it sufficeth us (John 14:8 KJV).

We can never truly satisfy self. We just have to deny it. We have to die to self and place God and others ahead of self. That's easier said than done, but once we die to ourselves, happiness is what we get.

Second, we need to deal with what's outside, our circumstances. Paul gave great insight into how to do that:

For our light affliction, which is but for a moment, worketh for us a far more exceeding and eternal weight of glory;
While we look not at the things which are seen, but at the things which are not seen: for the things which are seen are temporal; but the things which are not seen are eternal (2 Cor. 4:17–18 KJV).

Paul said his affliction was only light. He didn't say that because he didn't have problems. You can read a list of his "light afflictions" in **2 Corinthians 11:23–30**. The list includes beatings with whips and rods, prison, shipwreck, hunger and thirst because of his mission work, and many other problems. So, how can we speak about our heavy load when Paul called all his problems, which were much worse than anything we have suffered, just light afflictions?

You see, it's not your problems that are the problem. It's the way you see your problems and the value you place on them that makes them a problem. Paul said all his afflictions were but for a moment. He was saying they were short-lived compared to eternity. Paul put everything into the perspective of eternity.

Regardless of how bad things are in this life, we have such a wonderful eternity promised to each of us that all our troubles pale in comparison.

> **For I reckon that the sufferings of this present time are not worthy to be compared with the glory which shall be revealed in us (Rom. 8:18 KJV).**

Our future is so bright. All the sufferings of this life are short and insignificant compared to eternity and all the pleasures the Lord has in store for us. Keeping this in mind will shrink our problems down to a manageable size.

True Joy and Happiness are not Circumstantial

Paul also said in **2 Corinthians 4:18** that he didn't look at the temporary things of earth but that he was focused on the eternal things of heaven.

> **If we are only looking for happiness in this life, then we are going to be miserable (1 Cor. 15:19 NLT).**
> **Our true happiness lies in Jesus and our future with Him. If we are in faith, we can have joy unspeakable and full of glory now, in this life (1 Pet. 1:8 NLT).**
> **It's our anchor in eternity that keeps our hearts from being troubled (John 14:1–3 NLT).**

Circumstances control most people's happiness. But that's the problem: true joy and happiness don't come from circumstances.

Praising God is a Key that Unlocks God's Treasures

The apostle Paul gave us a great example of this. He had a vision from God that he was supposed to go minister to the people in Macedonia.

> **And a vision appeared to Paul in the night; there stood a man of Macedonia, and prayed him, saying, Come over into Macedonia, and help us.**

And after he had seen the vision, immediately we endeavored to go into Macedonia, assuredly gathering that the Lord had called us for to preach the gospel unto them (Acts 16:9–10 KJV).

Even though Paul and his companion, Silas, had a divine mandate from God to go and minister there, everything didn't go perfectly. Within just a few days, they were beaten and thrown in the worst part of the prison, with their feet and hands in stocks **(Acts 16:16–24)**. But Paul and Silas's response to this was praise.

And at midnight Paul and Silas prayed, and sang praises unto God: and the prisoners heard them (Acts 16:25 KJV).

This is great! After the awful treatment these two men endured, they were giving thanks—praying and singing praises unto God. They were so loud, in fact, that the other prisoners could hear them. They weren't just listening with their physical ears; they were listening with their hearts. Their praise ministered to the prisoners. When was the last time your praise in a terrible situation ministered to someone?

The prisoners were so blessed by Paul and Silas that when an earthquake came and the prison doors were opened and all of the chains fell off, none of them left.

And suddenly there was a great earthquake, so that the foundations of the prison were shaken: and immediately all the doors were opened, and everyone's bands were loosed.
And the keeper of the prison awaking out of his sleep, and seeing the prison doors open, he drew out his sword, and would have killed himself, supposing that the prisoners had been fled. But Paul cried with a loud voice, saying, Do thyself no harm: for we are all here (Acts 16:26–28 KJV).

Paul and Silas's praise released God's power. You see, praise to God blesses you, blesses others, drives away the devil, and blesses God. When you find yourself in an adverse situation and you offer genuine praise to God, you put yourself in a position to receive from Him! *Praise is a key that unlocks God's treasures.*

Paul wrote under the inspiration of the Holy Spirit to **"rejoice in the Lord always: and again I say, Rejoice" (Phil. 4:4 KJV).** This is such a radical concept, and I believe it's the reason he repeated it. He didn't want anyone to think this was a mistake. Rejoicing is a command.

Happiness is a State of Mind, not a State of Being

The whole world needs to hear this. People are doing everything within their power to be happy, but it's still elusive to most. **True joy can be found only in the Lord (Ps. 16:11).**

The scripture says, **"I will bless the Lord at all times" (Ps. 34:1a).**

Note that it says "all times." That means you can rejoice when circumstances are good and when they aren't. You can look at people who appear to have the ideal circumstances—politicians, movie stars, athletes, and the like. They have plenty of money, fame, recognition, and even the praises of some people. Many idolize them. Yet while they're in possession of everything in the natural world, many of them are miserable. They aren't happy people. I'm telling you, happiness is not dependent on circumstances or things. *It is a state of mind, not a state of being.* Paul understood this. Some people have never thought of him as a happy person because of all the terrible circumstances he endured, but he was. He knew the secret to happiness.

Most Christians believe that praising God and being thankful is good. However, many think it is optional, something to do after they have served the Lord in other ways. Some Christians praise God only when their circumstances are good and they have a reason to thank Him. The truth is that praising God is not an option. Praise has a powerful effect on the believer, on the devil, and on God. It is our highest calling.

Praising God Always - The key to happiness and Joy

How does praise affect the believer? When we praise God, we are acknowledging that it is not our own efforts that produce blessings and prosperity. In **Deuteronomy 7 and 8**, the children of Israel are told to remember to thank God for the abundance they will receive. God, not their own efforts, gave them wealth. Praise makes us humble.

Thanksgiving is also a way to abound in faith. Anytime we operate with a high degree of faith, praise is present.

> **As ye have therefore received Christ Jesus the Lord, so walk ye in him: rooted and built up in him, and stablished in the faith, as ye have been taught, abounding therein with thanksgiving (Col. 2:6–7 KJV).**

When you are believing in God for something and it is completed, praise is a natural response. What some people often fail to understand is that they can increase their faith with praise, and their answers will come more quickly.

By focusing on your problems instead of praising God, you become self-centered and prideful. Praise forces you to get your attention on God and off your problems. Some people say they are praying, but they are so focused on their problems that they are actually complaining. If you focus on the Word of God, faith will come. How do you keep from focusing on the problem when you are in pain or have no money? The most important thing you can do is praise God. A negative, complaining attitude won't change overnight, but beginning to praise God will start the transformation in your attitude. If you have always been negative, you must practice thinking on positive things. **Philippians 4:4** tells us to **"rejoice in the Lord always: and again I say, rejoice."**

When we pray, we should begin with praise and end with praise. The Lord's model for prayer (which most people call the Lord's Prayer) gives us this example, and we are also told this:

Be careful for nothing; but in everything by prayer and supplication with thanksgiving let your requests be made known unto God.
And the peace of God, which passeth all understanding, shall keep your hearts and minds through Christ Jesus (Phil. 4:6–7 KJV).

When you pray with thanksgiving, the peace of God will keep your heart and mind.

Praise will build you up spiritually and keep you from crumbling, "for the joy of the Lord is your strength" **(Neh. 8:10)**. The apostle Paul was persecuted and suffered far more than most of us, yet he put it all in perspective:

For our light affliction, which is but for a moment, worketh for us a far more exceeding and eternal weight of glory;
While we look not at the things which are seen, but at the things which are not seen: for the things which are seen are temporal; but the things which are not seen are eternal (2 Cor. 4:17–18 KJV).

Paul said that our affliction is just for a moment in light of eternity. He looked into the spiritual realm. Praise will push you into the spiritual realm to see what God has done for you. As you already know, Paul and Silas praised God in prison. It was the praise that released the power of God and the earthquake that delivered them from their captivity.

Praising God doesn't just affect us; it is a powerful weapon against the devil as well. **Psalm 8:2 says, "Out of the mouth of babes and sucklings hast thou ordained strength because of thine enemies, that thou mightest still the enemy and the avenger."** In the book of **Matthew (21:16)**, at the time of the triumphal entry into Jerusalem (Palm Sunday), Jesus quotes from **Psalm 8**. When he quoted this verse, he interchanged the words "perfected praise" for "ordained strength." This is a tremendous revelation: praise is strength **(Neh. 8:10)**!

Some people are so involved in spiritual warfare that their attention is on the devil more than on God. There is a place for fighting and resisting the devil, but focusing too much on the devil is not good. Praise is a powerful weapon against the devil that has no negative fallout. In **2 Chronicles 20**, Jehoshaphat appointed singers to lead his army into battle with praise unto the Lord. When they went into battle singing and praising God, the Lord set an ambush, and their enemies were defeated.

Why does praise defeat Satan? Satan's sin was jealousy of God. He is still driven by jealousy today **(Isa. 14:13–14)**. Even if he can't get people to worship him, his goal is to keep people from worshipping God. He seeks to draw attention away from God. When we worship God, we thwart Satan's plan. Praise makes the devil flee and releases the anointing of God. Even the secular world knows the benefits of praise.

The most important reason to praise God is that it ministers to Him. **Acts 13** describes a situation at the church in Antioch:

As they ministered to the Lord, and fasted, the Holy Ghost said, Separate me Barnabas and Saul for the work whereunto I have called them (Acts 13:2 KJV).

This is an awesome statement. They ministered to the Lord. How do we minister to the Lord? We often think we serve God only by ministering to other people. This happened in **Matthew 8**, with Peter's mother-in-law. She waited on them and did household duties. That is a ministry; however, in this instance in Acts, they were fasting, praying, and ministering to the Lord. They were worshipping and glorifying God. That also ministers to the Lord.

The truth is that God desires ministry. God is complete and self-contained, but He needs us to love Him. Any person who loves has a need to show that love and a need to have that love returned. That is the reason for the creation of humanity in the first place. In **Revelation 4**, John saw a vision of what is happening in heaven. He saw twenty-four elders and four living creatures that don't cease praising God. In **verse 11**, the elders say, **"Thou art worthy, O Lord, to receive glory and honor and power: for**

thou hast created all things, and for thy pleasure they are and were created." This tells us that God's original and current purpose for creation is for His pleasure. God created us to be full of praise, joy, and thanksgiving. He is blessed by His creation.

We are often so service oriented that we think we have to minister to others or work at church to bless God. We think our net worth to God is our service. We forget that if it blesses God, it doesn't have to touch anyone else. He longs to know us personally and intimately. Service is not a substitute for a relationship with God.

Our number-one priority must be to love God personally. Praise is giving of yourself to God—an intimate communion with Him. If we would praise and seek God first, during our prayer time, other things would be added unto us **(Matt. 6:33)**.

John 3:16 tells us that God gave His son that we might have eternal life. Christians often think eternal life begins when you die and go to heaven, but **John 17:3** tells us differently. Eternal life is now. Intimately knowing God is eternal life. Praise is a way to begin this love relationship with God.

By him therefore let us offer the sacrifice of praise to God continually, that is, the fruit of our lips giving thanks to his name (Heb. 13:15 KJV).

Praising God under all circumstances will bring happiness and joy into your life.

Chapter Sixteen

Closing

What to do When you Doubt that you can Start a Successful Business Without Money and Enjoy Financial Freedom and Happiness

Do you doubt that you can start a successful business without money and enjoy financial freedom and happiness? If you do, you're not alone because no one is immune to doubt. It can and does happen to us all. You've just got to know how to handle it when it comes. Never voice your doubt; rather voice what you want to see happen in your life, say only what the Word of God says concerning you. It's that simple. Everyday- people and even great men of God recorded in the Bible had to also deal with doubt. The list includes Abraham, Moses, Gideon, Jeremiah, Naaman, and John the Baptist.

For each of them who doubted, God simply told them I am with you. Today it's even better because the spirit of God lives in us and we also have the written Word of God. All their excuses sounded like "I don't have the money needed so I cannot start a successful business without money." See below for yourself:

Abraham: "Then Abraham fell upon his face, and laughed, and said in his heart, shall a child be born unto him that is a hundred years old? And shall Sarah, that is ninety years old bear?" Genesis 17:17(KJV)

Moses: "And Moses said unto the LORD, o my Lord, I am not eloquent, neither heretofore, nor since thou hast spoken unto thy

servant: but I am slow of speech, and of a slow tongue." Exodus 4:11 (KJV)

Naaman: "But Naaman was wroth, and went away, and said, Behold, I thought, He will surely come out to me, and stand, and call on the name of the LORD his God, and strike his hand over the place, and recover the leper." 2 Kings 5:11 (KJV)

Gideon: "And he said unto him, oh my Lord, wherewith shall I save Israel? Behold, my family is poor in Manasseh, and I am the least in my father's house." Judges 6:15 (KJV)

Jeremiah: "Then said I, Ah, Lord God! Behold, I cannot speak: for I am a child."Jer. 1:6 (KJV)

Jesus said of John the Baptist:

"Verily I say unto you, Among them that are born of women there hath not risen a greater than John the Baptist." Matt 11:11 (KJV)

That means John was greater in the eyes of Jesus than Abraham, Joseph, Moses, Gideon, David, Jeremiah or any Old Testament character you can name. Yet John doubted the most important thing of all by questioning whether Jesus was really the Christ.

He asked two of his disciples to go to Jesus and ask Him if He really was the Christ. It's easy to read that and not think much about it, but the truth is, it was nothing but unbelief on the part of John the Baptist. John is the one who saw Jesus and said, **"Behold the Lamb of God, which taketh away the sin of the world." John 1:29 (KJV)**

Thousands of people from many nations came to the middle of nowhere to hear this man preach, **"Repent ye; for the kingdom of heaven is at hand."Matthew 3:2 (KJV).** God had revealed to him that through a visible sign from heaven he would know who the Christ was. He would see the spirit of God descending upon the Messiah in bodily shape as a dove. That came to pass when John baptized Jesus in the Jordan River.

At that time, John was absolutely certain that Jesus was the Christ. He had zero doubt. He was so adamant about it that he said:

"I saw, and bare record that this is the Son of God" John 1:34 (KJV). In **Luke 3:16** he said, **"One mightier than I cometh, the latchet**

of whose shoes I am not worthy to unloose." And in **John 3:30** he said, "**He must increase, but I must decrease.**"

However, after being imprisoned for a period of time, he began to doubt. This says a number of things, but an important one is the fact that anyone can doubt. How did Jesus respond to John's doubt?

Jesus answered and said unto them in **Matthew 11:4–6**, "**Go and shew John again those things which ye do hear and see: The blind receive their sight, and the lame walk, the lepers are cleansed, and the deaf hear, the dead are raised up, and the poor have the gospel preached to them. And blessed is he, whosoever shall not be offended in me.**"

Notice that what Jesus told John the Baptist is exactly what is written in **Isaiah 35:5–6**: "**Then the eyes of the blind shall be opened, and the ears of the deaf shall be unstopped. Then shall the lame man leap as a hart, and the tongue of the dumb sing: for in the wilderness shall waters break out, and streams in the desert.**"

Jesus referred John the Baptist back to that Word of God. Jesus reminded John of the scriptures, to deal with his doubts. That is Jesus's method of dealing with our doubts.

"**We have also a more sure word of prophecy; Whereunto ye do well that ye take heed, as unto a light that shineth in a dark place, until the day dawn, and the day star arise in your hearts: Knowing this first, that no prophecy of the scripture is of any private interpretation.**" (2 Pt. 1:19–20 KJV)

The only sure way to overcome doubt is to place your faith in the Word of God. Don't allow your five senses to dominate your thinking. You must come to a place where God's Word is more real to you than anything you can see, taste, hear, smell, or feel. When you're in doubt, refer back to the Word of God just the way Jesus told John the Baptist to do. Faith comes by hearing and hearing by the Word of God.

There is a greater blessing from believing God's Word than there is from believing because of supernatural circumstances. Those who are looking for circumstances to confirm their faith will fail when the strong battles of unbelief come.

God's way for us to deal with the temptation to not believe is to get back to His best, which is His written Word. So whenever you're in doubt, get back to the Word of God and accept what it says about that situation.

The highest form of faith is faith that takes God at His Word. Just like the Roman centurion who said to Jesus: **"But speak the word only, and my servant shall be healed. For I am a man under authority, having soldiers under me: and I say to this man, Go, and he goeth; and to another, Come, and he cometh; and to my servant, Do this, and he doeth it." (Matthew 8:8–9 KJV)**

The centurion had a faith that was in God's Word alone. He didn't have to have Jesus come to his house and wave His hand over the sick servant. All he needed was the Word of Jesus. God expects us to do the same today. Do you doubt that you can start a successful business without money and enjoy financial freedom and happiness? Make up your mind today to overcome such doubt by getting back to the Word of God and say aloud to yourself only what the Word of God says concerning you. Remember what Jesus said in **Mark 9:23: "If thou canst believe, all things are possible to him that believeth." (KJV)**

Contrary to what many people believe, your most important asset in starting a successful business is not money but your tongue. **Proverbs 18:21: "Death and life are in the power of the tongue: and they that love it shall eat the fruit thereof." (KJV)**

It's sad when people are not careful with their words. Imagine someone who keeps saying, "I just don't see how I can make it as an entrepreneur without start-up capital; nothing seems to be working for me." You should never talk like that. If that has been your experience, it doesn't mean your experience should control you. Don't voice the negatives. This applies in every area of your life. **2 Corinthians 4:13: "We having the same spirit of faith, according as it is written, I believe and therefore have I spoken; we also believe and therefore speak." (KJV)**

Your speech dictates the circumstances of your life. If you say you can't be a successful entrepreneur because of lack of finances, it shall be so. Your speech should be consistent with what you want to see in your life. More than anything else, the main reason many entrepreneurs are not doing well in business is because they don't talk right. One can be very skillful, talented and intelligent and still fail in business or in life because of wrong confessions.

Zechariah 4:6–7: "Then he answered and spake unto me, saying, This is the word of the LORD unto Zerubbabel, saying, Not by might, not by power, but by my spirit, saith the LORD of hosts. Who are thou, o great mountain? Before Zerubbabel thou shalt become a plain: and he shall bring forth the headstone thereof with shoutings, crying, Grace, grace unto it."

Some people, because of their experience in life, would say, "You know, things can't just be rosy all the time. You win some, you lose some; sometimes up, sometimes down."

A Christian shouldn't talk like that. You're born to win always! You're built for success; it's part of your makeup. Talk that way!

Zechariah 4:9: "The hands of Zerubbabel have laid the foundation of this house; his hands shall also finish it; and thou shalt know that the LORD of hosts hath sent me unto you."

Refuse to be defeated! Refuse to be weak! Get yourself together and declare, "I'm a success! I was born to reveal the glory of God! My life is upward and forward only!" You must control the circumstances of your life with your tongue. Don't wait; start it now if you've not been doing it.

Your mouth was given to you to chart your course in life. If your words are disorderly your life will go in that direction; if your words are excellent, your life will go accordingly, as well.

The character of your words is the character of your personality. So, watch your words!

No man was ever better than his words; your life is the expression, the manifestation, and the reflection, of your words. Words define your life and your value and this applies to your business life, as well.

Hebrews 13:5–6: "Let your conversation be without covetousness; and be content with such things as ye have for he hath said, I will

never leave thee, nor forsake thee. So that we may boldly say, The Lord is my helper, and I will not fear what man shall do unto me." (KJV)

Romans 10:6–12: "But the righteousness which is of faith speaketh on this wise, Say not in thine heart, Who shall ascend into heaven? (that is, to bring Christ down from above) Or, who shall descend into the deep? (that is, to bring up Christ again from the dead) But what saith it? The word is nigh thee, even in thy mouth, and in thy heart: that is, the word of faith, which we preach. That if thou shalt confess with thy mouth the Lord Jesus, and shalt believe in thine heart that God hath raised him from the dead, thou shalt be saved. For with the heart man believeth unto righteousness; and with the mouth confession is made unto righteousness. For the scripture saith, Whosoever believeth on him shall not be ashamed." (KJV)

You do not need your own money to start a successful business, but most businesses will need money at some point. If the business idea—the gap you've seen in the market—is strong, it will attract the money it needs to grow from business angels, venture capital, banks, family members, and friends. However, note that sometimes money is overrated and there is *always* responsibility that comes with investors' money. What may seem like easy money is sometimes filled with major headaches and not worth it in the long run.

Don't let the lack of money prevent you from realizing your God-given business idea, but rather trust God to make a way for you. God is more concerned about your success in business than you can ever be for yourself. The reason is because He loves you unconditionally. You just need to have faith (put your trust) in Him.

Why You Must Be Born Again.

John 8:44 says: "Ye are of your father the devil, and the lusts of your father ye will do: he was a murderer from the beginning, and abode not in the truth, because there is no truth in him. When he speaketh a lie, he speaketh of his own: for he is a liar, and the father of it."

From the above scripture you can see that anyone who is not born again has a nature of sin. All of us were born in sin and were therefore "by nature" the children of the devil. That's the reason we sinned. Our sins don't corrupt our nature, but our corrupt nature makes us sin. A man is not a sinner because he sins rather a man sins because he is a sinner by nature. He is first of all a sinner before he ever sinned. That's why we must be "born again" and become new creatures (or a new creation) in Christ.

The scriptures teach that everyone was born with a sin nature or old man. For the Christian, the old man is dead. We do not have a nature that is driving us to sin. If that is the case, then why do we seem so bound to sin even after we experience the new birth? The reason is that our old man left behind what **Romans 6:6** calls a body. Just as a person's spirit and soul leave behind a physical body at death, so our old man left behind habits and strongholds in our thoughts and emotions. The reason a Christian tends to sin is because of an unrenewed mind, not because of a sin nature.

Our old man ruled our thinking before we were born again. He taught us such things as selfishness, hatred, greed and fear and he placed within us the desire for sin. The old man is now gone, but these negative parts of his body remain. Until renewed with the word of God, our minds continue to lead us on the course that our old man charted. Yes we are new creatures that never existed before but this is in our spirits. The resurrection of Jesus Christ made this possible for us but the new man came along with it our body and our mind. We must renew them with the word of God to conform to our born again spirit.

To experience the resurrection life of Jesus, we have to know that our old man is dead. Then, through the renewing of our minds, we destroy the body that the old man left behind. The end result is that we will not serve sin any longer. This is the man that overcomes the world.

For whatsoever is born of God overcometh the world: and this is the victory that overcometh the world, *even* **our faith. (1 Jn. 5:4 KJV)**

Do not be deceived except you are born again, you cannot win – you can never have total victory and peace of mind - because the one that is in the world (the devil with his demons) is greater than you. They've been around a long time before you came into this world. He will try to frustrate you in your business, health, marriage, relationship, family, job, etc. But if you're born again the Bible says: **"Ye are of God, little children, and have overcome them: because greater is he that is in you, than he that is in the world." (1Jn. 4:4 KJV)**

Nay, in all these things we are more than conquerors through him that loved us. (Rm. 8:37 KJV) Notice that our victory is through Him that loved us not through our performance or effort. We only need to believe in His love for us and what He has already done for us. You only need to believe the above sovereign declarations of the almighty God and they will work for you in your life.

The Most Important Decision of Your Life

Note that the most important decision of your life is this: **What shall I do with Jesus?** If you choose to accept Him by receiving the free gift of everlasting life He has offered you for free, your eternal destiny and your life on Earth will be glorious and quite different from what you will have if you choose not to accept Him.

"But if you are unwilling to serve the Lord, then choose today whom you will serve, would you prefer the gods your ancestors served beyond the Euphrates? Or will it be the gods of the Amorites in whose land you now live? But as for me and my family we will serve the Lord."(Joshua 24:15 NLT)

"For God so loved the world, that he gave his only begotten son, that whosoever believeth in him should not perish, but have everlasting life. For God sent not His Son into the world to condemn the world; but that the world through Him might be saved. He that believeth in Him is not condemned but he that believeth not is condemned already, because he hath not believed in the name of the only Son of God." (John 3:16–18 KJV)

Following God and believing in His Son, Jesus Christ, is a decision that has eternal implications.

I believe you have been blessed by this book, do you know where you will spend eternity? If you're not sure, you can be right now. If you're not born again I invite you, today, to make Jesus Christ the Lord of your life and receive His free gift of everlasting life to you by confessing as follows:

According to **Acts 2:21: "Whosoever shall call on the name of the Lord shall be saved,"** and **Romans 10:9: "If thou shalt confess with thy mouth the Lord Jesus, and shalt believe in thine heart that God hath raised Him from the dead, thou shall be saved."**

Confession: I confess the Lord Jesus with my mouth, and I believe that God raised Him from the dead. I ask Jesus to come into my heart, now, to be the Lord of my life. I receive everlasting life into my spirit. I declare that I am saved. I am born again. I am a child of God.

If you prayed the above prayer, congratulations! You are now born again because this is the Bible way to be born again. You now have everlasting life in your spirit man.

But without the Holy Spirit you cannot live a victorious Christian life. **"He said unto them, have ye received the Holy Ghost since ye believed? And they said unto him, We have not so much as heard whether there be any Holy Ghost." (Acts 19:2 KJV)**

So receive the Holy Spirit now by confessing as follows: I receive the Holy Spirit into my spirit in Jesus's name, Amen.

This is according to **Acts 1:8 KJV:**

"But ye shall receive power, after the Holy Ghost is come upon you: and ye shall be witnesses unto me both in Jerusalem, and in all Judaea, and in Samaria, and unto the uttermost part of the earth."(KJV)

If you said those prayers, you are now born again with the power of God (Holy Spirit) inside you. It's that simple. You don't have to feel anything. It's real because the word of God said so and God cannot lie. If you made the confession, the Holy Spirit lives in you right now. Please, from today forward, take advantage of who lives in you now and keep saying only what you want to see in your life, your business, and in the life of your loved ones as you have learned in this book. And watch how everything about you will transform gloriously before your eyes. I encourage you to study God's Word like never before and also attend a Bible-believing church where only the unconditional love of God and the grace of God are preached. You need only to believe in what Jesus Christ has already done for you because of His unconditional love for you. You will experience the miraculous hand of God in your life and become a witness for Jesus Christ by testifying to others what God has done in your life because of your believe in Jesus. This is what God wants from you – to be a witness of the goodness and unconditional love of God based on your personal relationship with Jesus so that others can also be blessed and win in life through your testimony.

You are the blessed, the helped, and the prospered in Jesus's name. Amen.

References

Applegate, Jane. *201 Great Ideas for Your Small Business*. Hoboken, NJ: Bloomberg Press, 2011.

Holy Bible, New Living Translation (NLT).

Holy Bible, King James Version (KJV).

Lechter, Michael A. *OPM—Other People's Money: How to Attract Other People's Money for Your Investments. The Ultimate Leverage*. New York: Business Plus, 2005.

Lester, David. *How They Started—How Thirty Good Ideas Became Great Businesses*. Bath, UK: Crimson Publishing, 2007.

Rhapsody of Realities, www.rhapsodyofrealities.org.

Waitley, Daris. *The Power of Resilience*.

Andrew Wommack Ministries, www.awmi.net.

www.Startups.co.uk.

www.wikihow.com

The Richest Man in Babylon, by George S. Clason, Publisher Penguin Books, Originally published in 1926.

You can't beat God givin': Miracle testimonies from ordinary people serving an extraordinary God, by R.W Schambach. Paperback-1994.

www.ingramcontent.com/pod-product-compliance
Lightning Source LLC
Chambersburg PA
CBHW051911170526
45168CB00001B/333